Biking,
Sailing,
Climbing and Crawling,
Gallivanting,
Traipsing,
and otherwise
Journeying
through Life
and
A Winter
On Torch Lake
By

John Chuchman

Additional copies of this book
And copies of the author's other titles
"Springtime in Autumn,"
"Pebbles of Wisdom,"
"Quest," and
"Sunset Awakening"
may be ordered from Booksurge.com
or from the author at

poetman@freeway.net
http://my.freeway.net/~poetman

Contents

Biking and Sailing
(And Otherwise Journeying)
Through Life

Written in 1988-1992

A Winter on Torch Lake

Written in 1993-4

Views Along the Way

Written in 2003-2004

Preface

With the success of my previously written works,
I was motivated to share
some of my earlier
unpublished writings.

Much of Biking Through Life was written
During my five years in Lancaster County,
Pennsylvania,
When I biked over 25,000 miles
through some truly beautiful countryside.

A Winter on Torch Lake was written
During my three months of solitude
contemplation and self-discovery
on Beautiful Torch Lake, Michigan.

So that this book would include
Not only "old" stuff,
I conclude the offering
with some of my recent writings
as Views Along Life's Journey.

I owe much to many who are inspiration
and encouragement to me,
But I owe a special Thank You
To Martha Williams
Who
despite a thoroughly busy life,
re-transcribed my old works.

My Love

Beloved,
I know how difficult it is for you to Love Me,
A God you cannot see,
a God you cannot touch.
So Love Me in your brothers and sisters,
My children.
Love them All and Love them
Without Condition,
for Love is Divine.

Everyone of you who Loves,
confirms that you are My Child and
that I am your Father.
Everyone of you who Loves, knows Me.

You who don't Love,
don't know Me;
and no matter
how well-intentioned your actions,
without Love, they mean nothing to Me;
they have no value to Me without Love,
for *I am Love*.

I don't keep My Love a Secret.
I show it to you in the following way;
I send you My Only Divine Son
into the suffering world
so that You may live Eternally.

What is True Love?
You are not yet fully capable of True Love;
even your Love of God.
True Love is My Son Atoning for your sins.
You must seek True Love
by Loving one another
in the same way that I Love you.
This is True Love.

No one has seen Me,
but when you Love one another
(All and Without Condition),
I live in your heart and
My Love, Perfect in its Giving,
is perfected by you
in its receiving.

The way you know that I live in your heart
and that you dwell in Me,
is through
My Holy Spirit.

You can see for yourselves and you must testify
that I send My Son as the Savior of the world.

When you acknowledge,
not only in word, but also in deed,
that Jesus is My Son,
I dwell in you,
and you in Me.

You can know and you can rely on
the Love I have for you.

I am Love,

When you live in Love,
You live in Me
and
I in You.

1 John 4, 7-16

Biking and Sailing (and otherwise Journeying) Through Life

Biking Through Life

Which way to go, O Lord?
What trail shall I Bike today?
Don't really know where to head,
just know that I have to Bike.

Your hills are sometimes tough to climb,
but the view, once on top,
makes it all worthwhile.
...and gliding down is so much fun.

Your wind often makes peddling so very hard
but my muscles grow with the experience,
and that very wind, once at my back,
pushes me along so joyfully.

Your rain, that feeds the thirsty earth,
sometimes dampens my desire to Bike,
but it does so cool my sweated brow,
and brings to me Your glorious rainbow.

Biking through life brings so many joys,
the chance to really see
the things You've given:
flowers, trees, sky,
creatures large and small,
the sounds of birds and crickets and kids,
the smells of blossoms... and of pigs.

Biking through life gives me
the time and
the space
to enjoy the trip.

And oh those forks and crossroads,
Which way to go, O Lord?

To relocate or to stay put,
to work at business or do Your work,
to meditate or to praise out loud,
to sell this and keep that,
to study or to teach,
...so many forks
...so many crossroads.

But if Biking through life
is, in fact, the joy,
if seeing – and enjoying – all that You've given
us,
along the way,
is really what it's all about,
and not a matter of getting to a certain place
in a certain way,
in a specified time,

then, I'll simply Bike on...
try a fork in the road here,
cross a road there,
climb a hill to the East,
face a wind to the West,
follow my instincts,
listen to Your call.

And even though I may or may not pass this
way again,
or take a turn I missed before;
It makes no difference,

as long as I see all there is to see is You,

and

help any stranded Bikers along the way.

An Early Spring is Sprung

Spring's early this year.

Birds are chirping, grass greening,
buds blooming, kids cavorting.

So nice to see life start again,
sooner than expected.

Skies are blue, shirt sleeves
(and skirts) short,
people happy, farmers hopeful.

Everything'll go right this season.

The Bikers are bikin', Joggers joggin',
Walkers walkin', Dreamers dreamin'

Time to fix and clean; it's fun.

Trees to prune, car to wax,
windows to wash, garage to clean.

Only good news:

Nature's free, kids are healthy,
Food is plentiful, God is good.

Nothing at all could spoil this joy – except...

New Life in Chicago in the '40's

The excitement of being awaken in darkness
earlier than ever before.

The pride in putting on this Easter's new suit
and shiny new shoes.

The chill walking to church earlier than
anyone else to get the incense ready and
put on the cassock and altar boy garb.

The thrill of hearing the St. Nicholas Choir
herald the resurrection and welcome
parishioners to church.

The joy in being part of the church
procession circling St. Nicholas three
times to the toll of the grand church
bells.

The tears brought on by the entire Parish
singing the Risen Christ's Resurrection.

The fatigue associated with assisting at
services lasting over two and a half
hours.

The exhilaration of running two blocks to
Grandma's house for Easter Breakfast
with relatives assembled.

The mouth watering smell of Punchkies and
Kielbasa,

The taste of Boiled Eggs, Ham and
Horseradish.

The satisfying walk home in the Easter
Sunshine.

Easter Memories.

Choice

I thank God for all He has given me:
this beautiful earth on which to live,
food to eat and drink,
flowers to smell,
loving relationships,
...health.
Indeed, I treasure each and every new day –
each and every new moment....

But before me stands
an abyss.
An abyss so deep, I cannot see the bottom.
In fact, a cold dark, dense fog several feet out
prevents me from seeing across the abyss.
Turn away!
Treasure all that God has given you...

At my feet, stretching out across the deep
black hole into the fog is a line...
apparently crossing the abyss
through the fog to the other side.

Turn away!
It's a sacrilege to ignore all that God has
created for you... in search of?
The line jiggles and shakes!
Out of the fog, on the line, appears
a figure coming towards me.

Closer and closer He comes,
and finally I give my outstretched hand
to help Him reach my side.
"What's on the other side?" I ask.
"Come, I'll take you," He replies.
"Oh no, I couldn't."

"Don't you think I can cross it again?"
"I do, I do, but...
I don't think I can..."
"Come, I'll help, I'll carry you across."

(Give up all I know?
all the beauty on this side?
the birds? the flowers?
the fish in the sea, my friends?
all I've worked so hard to build?)

"Believe me, I can take you to where ...
....
.... Oh, it's really not possible to tell
you
in terms you'll understand...

Why not, simply,

Cross with ME...

Meditation

I dim the house lights,
try to hush the crowd,
in order to raise the curtain
on the Star.

The lights I can control and
the crowd noises eventually come down,
but getting to the Star seems
impossible.

So many many "warm-up" acts
want to perform,
to stay on-stage,
to steal the show,
to become the Star.

…sometimes the main event never gets on…

I keep trying,
dimming the lights, hushing the noise,
trying to keep the lesser acts
off-stage,
or at least get on and off quickly
so I can see the Star.

But the lesser acts are all my children,
I've sponsored them all,
they think they have a right
to be on-stage

...even if the Star never makes it...
The job, the children,
the car, the house,
sports,
problems with relatives,
health and wealth,
new furniture,
appliances,
toys,
all want the center stage,
the spotlight,
my conscious thought.
They're mine, why shouldn't they stay
front and center?

With uncharacteristic patience,
the Star simply waits back-stage,
never clamoring to get-on,
simply waiting
until I can get the house lights down,
the crowd noise silent,
and the many many pre-lim acts
over and done,
on and off,
out of the way,
so that I can truly see
the Star of the Show,
My God....

He patiently waits
in my backstage
until I can control
the lights and noise
until I can put aside
the acts that win only fleeting awards
to show me what the MAIN EVENT
is really all about.

Pity those who pay the ticket price,
and never see the Star.
He's there for every performance,
but rarely gets on stage.

Dim the lights, hush the noise,
raise the curtain...
Dim the lights, hush the noise,
See the Star.
Dim the lights, hush the noise.

Extra Innings

The game's not over.

Winter's late March rally has
sent the game to extra-innings.

April will surely witness the inevitable
victory of youth...

Winter's team is just too aged, too worn;
they'll never last.

But these vets don't die easy;
they're still pounding Spring
with frigid rain and sleet and icy fog...
(knucklers and spit balls).

Summer's sluggers
look nowhere to be found.

How long can this battle go on?

Send in the Relief Crew, Quickly!

Forty Days and Nights?

April showers bring May flowers;
but they need to stop long enough
for me to cut the grass that's
growing as well.

April showers help the farmers;
but when will they be able to
get the seed in the ground?

April showers help raise the water table;
but keep it out of my basement please.

April showers signal the coming of Summer;
or is it the beginning of the great deluge?

April showers are poetic;
but let's not make it an epic poem.

April showers end Old Man Winter's reign;
but one tyrant's rain is as bad as another's.

April showers...

better get out the Ark, Noah.

Hope

Is it there?

or despair?

Pat on the Back
Words "Well Done."
That's all it takes

PLUS

Give 'em all a

CHANCE TO FAIL

i.e. make mistakes.

HOPE?

Who knows...

The Games

Good news gets no play.
Read the papers and all one sees is
Bad News.
One person robbed, another murdered.
Storms wreak havoc, accidents maim.
Economies fail; governments fall.
Corruption, disruption, destruction.

Except for one section… Sports.

Although losses in Sports are tough
for the Fans;
They don't compare with the losses
of wealth, power, life and limb
found in the news.
And as opposed to the news,
In Sports, there is always good news,
Someone always wins.
Achievements are exceeded, Fun is had.
and even when one's team looses…
Tomorrow brings another chance.

The difference between life and the game?
Nothing really,
Life could be enjoyed like the games,
if the players only followed the rules.

Service

"Pokey" was her nickname, she told us,
but it certainly wasn't descriptive
of her drive and desire to please
her TWA Customers.

She bubbled, sparkled, smiled and laughed;
she served, charmed, befriended and scurried.

"Pokey" is Customer Satisfaction;
that little bit extra needed to please,
not just efficient, but concerned;
not just cheerful, but bubbly;
not just doing a job well; but
enjoying it too.

Was so pleased I dropped a note to TWA,
"Don't ever lose Leigh Ann;
all your attendants should be so
"Pokey."

Biking and Life

Route
Have I planned the route? Do I know
where I want to go? ...how far I want to
travel? ...what I want to see?
...considered the terrain? ...hills?
How long will the trip last?

Preparation
Do I have enough supplies? ...energy
food ? ...water? What's the weather?
Am I prepared for a change? Do I have
tools? ...spares?

Wind
At my back, I can really fly. Do I
conserve energy for return against it?
At my back, I get spoiled... it's so easy...
so quiet... so fast.

A beam, the wind is unsettling. It
threatens my control. It's harder to
keep a straight course. Hang on. It
gusts and is unpredictable. Wow,
almost off the road. Forget speed...
Keep control.

Head on, this is WORK. Keep low for aerodynamics... but straighten up to keep those lungs pumpin'. Hard work... wish I'd had the wind head on headin' out and at my back flyin' home. Pump, pedal, push, move through this wind... keep a steady pace.

Terrain
When it's flat, only the wind seems to matter... pace is my choice, speed is up to me. Not so scenic... but not so variable.

Curves add variety. How to take 'em? Broad? Sharp? Straight up? Slowly? At high speed? Straight up? Sloped? Curves add spice.

Up hill... gear down. Pick up speed at the start? Keep the pace? Gear down. ...getting harder. Gear down. Muscles working, lungs a pumpin' ...Gear down. Sweat, Heart a pumpin', dry throat... Gear down. Tough hill. Gear down and Bear down. Pace is good, but I do slow.

As I hit the top and Gravity eases and the pressure against the muscles skips away... so does apparent strength.

Over the crest a few moments of coasting allows the muscles to regain power.

Now the ride downhill. To pedal or coast. After. all that work uphill, why not reap the reward and coast down? No, pace is important. Keep pedaling. But I don't need the speed... but so much fun. Faster... faster... wind in the face. Down as low as possible... seems to mean more than pedaling. Wow! Faster and faster... don't lose control. Such exhilaration! T'was well worth the climb... but there's another climb ahead... so soon?

Weather
Cold crisp mornings... sunrises... warming rays and warm perspiration. Dawn lit crops, birds a chirpin'.

Hot summer days... tough humidity... drink some water—more.

Clouds... overcast... drizzle on my goggles in my face. Feels good. Now rain. Pull over? Keep goin'. Beat it home. I'm soaked. T'was fun being crazy.

Sunsets, colors... beat the dark.

Mix

Wow! Hills and wind and curves and sun.

Uphill and wind abeam and drizzle.

Downhill wind at my back and sun a setting.

Do a long long loop and see it all.

Covered bridges, discourteous drivers, rabbits
and skunks and swans and pheasants.

Corn and rye and tobacco and grass.

City and village, town and farm, river and
creek and pond and stream.

Kids and farmers, housewives and truckers.

Biking is life; Life is Biking.

Plan your route... see it all... prepare yourself...
mix it up... enjoy it all.

The sun rises; the sun sets....

Perspective

Morning is God's time of day; night, the devil's.

At dawn there's hope, joy, the start of a new
opportunity;
at night, despair, sadness, darkness.

The sounds of morning are gentle; Night's
noises are harsh, cruel, brash and cold.

Morning smells of due and flowers and
breakfast;
Night smells are foul and trashy and smoky.

At Dawn,
anything can be accomplished that day;
the approaching darkness signals our failures.

The morning light intensifies as the day grows,
but evening and night slowly turn the blue to
black.

Blue: loyal and true; Blue: heavenly and royal.
Black: emptiness and blindness;
Black: sadness and mourning.

Day calls for action, for doing, for achieving;
we sleep in order that night's boredom
pass quickly.

Rebirth, new life, youth, a beginning: Day.

Old age, sorrow, ending, death: Night.

Night is for sure;
it always triumphs over Dawn and Day;

Dawn, not so sure;
will we awake from Night's hibernation?

Day? Night? Which is best?

They're simply life…

and death.

Married to whom?

Spending too long with a Corporation

gives it a life of its own,

interwoven with mine and very real.

My wife, my children, my dreams, my
achievements,

all impacted by the Corporation.

In a sense, it is all my fellow workers, whom

I like and enjoy;

But, really, it's not them at all, but

a life of its own.

Having devoted my life and career,

having devoted my work and my time,

I need only wait for the Corporation to

spit me out, sucked dry.

SRO

Ordinarily, knowing the ultimate outcome of
the contest
dulls one's interest in the battle.

Not so with Winter's defense against Summer's
onslaught
on Spring's playing field.

Even though confident Summer always wins,
the final
score recorded by bird and bud and baseball
is different every game.

Sometimes Team W fades in the early innings
but roars back for a final gasp;
or sometimes it freezes the S team out
through most of the game and
gradually melts away.

Each game is different, each team's players—
wind, snow, sleet, clouds, ice; sun, warmth,
birds, buds, color—
play different roles each time.

Though the final score is known by all, each
and every game
is sold out—and enjoyed by all.

Never to Return?

How to reverse the ripples
spiraling ever outward from the pebble
dropped.

How to gather the feathers
back into the pillow broken open.

How to coach the leaves
back onto the tree after the snows approach.

NOW I find out that the loving family
stays together and
helps each other work things out... long after.

I thought MOBILITY was what it was all about,
that leaving home to succeed on your own
was true success,
that everyone needed to do it on their own.

I have the LOVE (plenty), the time (not much),
some wisdom (more than before),
the sincere desire to help,
but the trouble is

The ripples have landed on distant shore,
the feathers have ridden their winds of fortune
far afield,

the leaves have changed their color and

here sit I, sunken pebble, shriveled pillow case,
old proud barren tree.

Cause of it all, I only hope that

a stray ripple bounces back,
though weaker than it was,

a loose feather floats home,
though weathered,

or at least

the new trees, fed by my leaves,
stand tall.

Magical March

Winter, fighting for its very life,

blowing icy winds across budding plants,
laying frost upon open fields,
chilling walkers to the bone.

Summer, anxious to get on stage,

setting a marvelous blue skyscape,
turning things green,
evoking thoughts of baseball.

Spring, caught in between,

taking showers - sometimes warm, others cold -
even frigid
running sap, sometimes frozen,
wearing boots and caps with short sleeve shirts
and shorts.

The titanic struggle, ferocious fading winter,
onrushing confident summer,
confused, yet hopeful spring

all battling headlong in marvelous turbulent
March.

What a wonderful time: Crisp - even icy -
mornings,

Sun shining brightly,

new life battling the frost, bikers,
golfers, baseball players overtaking skiers,

color coming back,

new life, new hope, new beginnings

overtaking old fears, tears, chills and spills

all in

magical March.

Poetry

The alphabet: letters,
nuts and bolts, clay, paint,
the raw material with which
to fashion the
Work of Art, the Masterpiece.

Prose: the essay, story, novel,
good: read once and enjoyed;
great: read once and maybe twice
and perhaps again in later life.

But Poetry:
Read in sunshine, reflecting its rays;
read in sorrow, providing soft comfort;
read in despair, urging fresh starts;
funny, sad, loving, inspiring;
all of these in poetry.

Ageless, timeless; always fresh, yet friendly,
Like Music, yet more personal
Like Painting, yet more personal
Like Sculpture, yet more personal
Poetry:
the Author and me,
communicating one on one
with his truth reaching me in a
thousand different rays depending on how

I hold his gem up to the Sun.

God blessed us

with four children.

I love 'em all so very much;

I see some of me in

Mark: Confident, self centered,
success driven.

Jacqueline: A good mind - and heart,
perhaps too much of a softy.

Matthew: Creative, sensitive,
sometimes rash.

Jerome: Pensive, thoughtful, deep,
still searching.

Do I know them better than they me?

Away from the nest, how can I learn more
about their needs and help fulfill them?

How can I give them more of a chance
to know me better than I knew

my Dad?

To pass this way again?

Biking through the Lancaster countryside;

What a joy?

Exploring back roads, Amish farms, covered
bridges;

How exhilarating!

Sunrises, wind in my face, spring showers,
glorious sunsets;

What inspiration!

To keep on trying to find new roads, new farms,
new views?

Or to go back over old trails

seeing them in new lights, new seasons,
new ways?

I guess exploring anew is great;

but after all, there are some real benefits in

recycling.

Letting Go

My Kids... like Kites... put together
with sweat, Loving care, and pride,
pulled along to get them off the ground,
picked up and patched after each fall,
removed from trees and telephone lines,
(and other obstacles)
eventually to soar and reach for the
Heavens.

My Kids... like Kites... reeled home
after each new adventure -- until
the pull becomes too tough to hold,
forcing their release (with Sweet Sorrow)
or the line that binds... abruptly breaks.

It's great to see my Kids... unlike Kites...
reach new heights... on their own... without
my pull or patch, but with my pride.

But why can't my Kids... unlike Kites...return...
to use their soaring skills
to lift me to the heights
of which I dreamed
when I was young?

It seems so sad that
Kids... like Kites...
need to go so far away to reach new heights
...especially when your eyesight starts to go.

Mélange

I remember as a kid
revulsing at the way older folks always
seemed to mix up all the food on their plate,
one vegetable with another with another
mixed with gravy, potatoes, rice or whatever.

Every time I questioned them,
the stock answer was
"It all goes down the same stomach, anyway."

Why as a youth did I need to keep all those
tastes and flavors separate and distinct?

Perhaps with no past, no history, I needed
to learn all these new tastes and classify
and catalog them in my own mind.

Perhaps I needed to taste and learn and savor
life's individual experiences.

It's funny how I now enjoy
mixing up all the foods
on my dish, trying one with another,
combining,
experimenting, seasoning, creating new tastes.

Maybe it's because I'm old enough
to have tasted
most of life's single flavors
and new ones only
come from combinations of the old.

Maybe it's because all my past experiences
seem to meld together anyway;

it's harder and harder to
single out individual thoughts, feelings, events.

Oh well, it all goes in the same stomach,
anyway.

God Is!

And not just in Heaven,
But here on Earth.

God exists in Me
and in each and every one of His children.

God is Love!

God abides on earth as Love,
Unconditional Love.

I Love!

I am capable of Loving,
even unconditionally.

I can Love God in me,
and in His Children.

In Unconditional Loving,
I experience God;
I become one with God.

God is... Love...
I Love... I am...
God is... Love... I Love... I am...
God... Is...

Second chances

Today biking, on the 48th of 50 miles,

I saw ahead of me a young boy
standing alongside the road
looking for my attention.

(I meditate and contemplate,
even pray
while biking,
trying to become a loving person.)

As I got closer,
I saw his sign and
his almost angelic, pleading, face,

"Ice Tea, 10 cents".

Something, someone,
in me
said stop,
Make his day, but
No,
I needed to complete my 50; besides,
who knows what's in the Ice Tea.

I passed -- with some regret and a
"No, thank you."

Hours later,
I felt like a fool.
What a simple beautiful way to show love,
have some tea,
make his day,
leave him a dollar, or five, or ten.
So easy... but I somehow needed to complete
a journey.

I jumped in my car,
went back to find him,
knowing he would not be there,
knowing the angelic pleading face
would be gone,

knowing, we rarely get second chances.

He was not there. I came home.

A nothing event, which taught me a lesson:
Don't pass up the spontaneous chance

To Love.

The chances are all around us,

they aren't necessarily pre-planned --
at least in our eyes --
and they may be one shot deals.

I will go back -- on my bike --
to look for
the young man,
asking "10 cents an ice tea",
to see if I can show some

Love.

If he's given up his Iced-Tea venture,

hopefully,
I'll get a second chance to show Him

Some Love.

Imagination

What is it that makes us different
than God's others?

Our tools? Our gatherings? Not our violence?
Caring for our young?
Our language or communication?

No, God's other species do these too.

Some say it's our ability to image... imagination,
to envision what was, what might be,
what could have been.

Some say, no other species on our planet
have this magic.
Magic, because it is envisioning,
it is the imagining of what might be,
that actually makes it happen.

And our species, with reckless abandon,
imagines great good and much evil
without a reckoning,
without
accountability.

We think imagination is merely a step along the
way to planning or doing,
but imagination, some say,
makes it happen.

This gift is only ours.

But, where does Love fit in?
Is this not far greater than imagination?
No other is capable of True Love
as is the human species.

Love must be the greater.

But how does Love relate to imagination?

True Love sees no faults, asks no Love in return,
is unconditional.

No object of our love can be that perfect,
can be Godlike.

No one on earth is without fault or frailty, yet,
there exists True Love on earth... Love which
sees no weaknesses,
which demands nothing in return.

Imagination it must be,
which enables us to see our Loved
One without fault or failing.

Imagination it must be,

which enables us to foresee a time when we
are Loved in return...
unconditionally.

Imagination, at a minimum, seems a gateway
to True Love.

But, in Loving unconditionally, It must be
something of God
we are envisioning (imagining)
in our Loved One.

But God IS Love.

By truly Loving another are we sharing
in some way
in God?

Is it imagination which allows us to see
something of God
here on earth?

Is it imagination
in seeing something of
God's perfection in another
which enables us to Love
unconditionally, to be "in Love",
to be "with God"?

Imagination is, indeed, significant,
in making us different,
but seemingly only a gateway for the greater
act of Loving.

Unless...

Imagining is, indeed, what makes it happen.

If imagination actualizes our Loving,
our relationship with God
here on earth...
it is what truly makes us different.

...if we choose to imagine goodness,
perfection, Godness,

...if we choose to Love another unconditionally
and thus
partake of God,

and if we don't, instead, imagine evil and
become one with...

We'd forgotten...

...Just how fast they move, walking or crawling.
Turn your back, blink your eyes, look away,
and they're gone...
up the stairs, down the stairs, into trouble.
...just how much attention they do require.
Little loving granddaughters of 4 and 1.
talking, playing, singing, dancing, crying,
wetting, sleeping, digging,
every single moment.

...just how beautiful and loving our daughter is.

Mature, sweet, gentle, attractive, loving,
just a great gal -- although we raised
ours a bit different and wonder why she can't
do it the way we did... Oh well.
...what two little tornadoes can do to an
over-fifty empty nest. Toys here, toys there,
clothes here, clothes there, books, strollers,
walkers, things out of place, things hidden,
now that they're gone, hose the place down,
...just how fast they grow...Christine's almost
walking, Catherine's vocabulary sometimes
stuns. Our kids never grew so fast.
...just how many photos one can take of one's
Grandkids.

Eating, playing, sleeping,
walking, talking, dancing... all on film.
...just how much fun it is for all us adults to
watch a one-year old dig in to her
Birthday cake. Slowly at first, gently
picking at some icing, a finger in here, a
finger in there, chocolate's good, now a
hand, grab a hunk, feed your face, what a
mess, so much fun all on film.
...how quiet it is after the storm. Time to sleep,
time to rest, chance to recover...

love 'em

twice...

comin' and goin'

...just how good God has been to us.

Thanks, God.

I used to think

that being *self-centered* was wrong.
that it was being selfish.

I now know
that being *self-centered* means
achieving a balance between

the material and   the spiritual,
the mental and   the emotional,
the analytical and   the creative,
the left brain and   the right brain.

I now know that being *self-centered*
means finding one's *true* self,

finding **God within me.**

Who am I?

All my life, I've tried to be the person others
expected me to be.

At first, it was my parents;
pleasing them kept me safe.

Then it was the nuns at St. Nicholas;
doing what they said, reaped rewards.

I worked hard to be one of the "guys";
"belonging" seemed important,

At Weber High, there was no question;
I needed to follow the rules to succeed.

In college, I had to be the person
GM expected;
they paid my way through school.

Pleasing my wife was so very important;
I love her so very much.

Being a good father to all my kids meant
being the kind of Dad I thought they expected
and needed.

Succeeding in the Ford World required
that I be the kind of corporate person they
expected.

My whole life,
working to be
who other people expected me to be.

Now, after 55 years,
those people who I let define John Chuchman
are gone or are living their own lives,
and no longer really care who I am.

What a surprise.
What a shock.

After all these years,
I wonder
who am I, really?

I only just now (after 55 years) found out
that I can be
the person I want to be,
the person God wants me to be,
(and that only when I do, can I be truly
happy).
AND I LIKE HIM!
AND I THINK GOD LIKES (LOVES) HIM TOO!

(Why did I wait so long?)

Pendulum

We can let the pendulum of Life
stay centered and motionless

to avoid the pain and sorrow
at one end of the arc.

But, in doing so,
we'll miss all the joys and ecstasies
at the other end.

(A clock whose pendulum doesn't swing
is rather useless, anyway.)

Famous People

Come--and just like us--go.

Some people think
the things that Famous People
say and do
are more important.

But are they more important
to us and those around us
than what we say and do?

Many people see and hear
what Famous people
say and do
because that's what
being Famous is.

But if I touch another,
heal his hurt,
mend her wound,
is it less important,
though less famous?

If what I say and do
is good,
and only I and one other and God know;
what I am or say or do
needs no fame,

only Love.

To Squeeze or not to squeeze...

Don't squeeze the grapes of life;
they look so beautiful glistening in the sunlight.

Don't take a bite of that luscious red apple;
a chunk removed spoils
its round red appearance.

Don't rip off that banana's skin;
its bright yellow garb is so appealing.

Not having tasted the fruit of life,
they might as well be
wax...

maybe they're wax anyway.

Oh well, if I wait around long enough, I'll be
able to tell
if they're real –
they'll rot.

...Better, after all, I think,
to have squeezed and bitten and tasted life,
than to admire counterfeits or to
simply sit and watch life's genuine fruit die

un-tasted.

Whirlpool

To jump into the whirlpool; to let go of all my
handholds, all the
things I've collected to make me feel secure to
have complete
faith and trust in my Creator knowing that His
Love for
me will see me through these trials that I now
face;
to accept the fact that I don't know where I'm
going or how I'm going to get there; to
jump in over my head; to accept the
rough journey, the dizziness,
the uncertainty; to ride His
flow; to go deeper and
deeper within; to
let go of all my
attachments;
to find my
God deep
inside
me.

Not enough time

Modern nutrition is really a whiz.
It works far better than I can recall.
Our kids grew healthy
although slowly it seems,
compared to my Grandkids
who have grown twice as fast.
My daughter, I ask,
"What do you feed 'em?"
Her recipe it seems
no different than ours.
Why is it, then, that they grow
by the minute?
Please slow up the pace
before We depart.
They shouldn't be rushing so fast
to gain their adulthood
to the time when only a memory
we'll be.
Please slow up the pace before
we depart.

Journey

I look down, but cannot see to the bottom,
if, indeed, there is one.
I can simply stay put and feel safe,
but the call seems for me to
jump.

Jump?
Into what?

Do I believe my soul's immortal?
Do I believe He will take care of me?
Do I trust in Him?
Can I leave all my "belongings" behind?
Is this the test of Faith?

I **do** believe.
I'll jump.
I have **Faith**.

Falling, falling, falling,
I'm tempted to grab onto a protruding branch.
Falling, falling, falling,
I'm tempted to grab onto a ledge
to catch my breath,
to see if I can see what's below,
to make sure I'll be ok,
to see if He's really going to take care of me,
because maybe I'm not so sure.

But I don't;

I Hope
He's here
taking care of me.
I don't grab onto an attachment,
I don't try to verify His concern for me,
I just keep falling, falling, falling,
hoping, hoping, hoping,
He'll guide me, hold me, catch me,
wherever I fall.

On the way down,
I see others,
some falling like me,
some hanging on without hope,
some not ready to jump with faith.
I judge them not,
I share my experience,
I tell them,
"Join me!"
I treat them all with compassion,
I even try to help them along
(without getting attached or hung-up myself).
I **Love** them all
and decide to

Truly Enjoy the Journey.

Insights

How surprising
that the many chance encounters and
seemingly coincidental events and
apparently random acts
which affect my life and guide me,
are all simply part of His Plan.

How revealing
that I am simply
the sum total of all my past experiences,
of all the past experiences of my ancestors,
of all of humanity.

How beautiful
is Creation with all the plants and animals,
and even the rocks,
radiating a marvelous energy,
just like us.

How shameful
that humans strive to energize themselves
by stealing the energies of other humans
by dominating them and controlling them
and manipulating them.

How truly energizing
is appreciating the beauty of creation and
truly loving others and energizing them,

thus tapping myself into the Universal Energy
available to all who do so.

How sad
that I have energized myself in the past
at the expense of others
by intimidating them and interrogating them,
and by acting as a "Poor Me" and an "Aloof,"
when all I needed to do was grow forward
from the place
where my parents brought me.

How amazing that all the answers
that I ever needed and will need
are all around me in the people I encounter
and that what I don't always know is the right
question.

How really helpful to be open to the messages
people give me
when I open myself to them
and share the deep profound personal truth in
me.

How wonderful
that we are evolving to the point
of harmony and fulfillment,
of awareness and intuition,
of true spirituality.

A Volunteer

Who am I to think that I might
console those in Grief?
They tell me that I can help
by simply listening and
caring.
Although I do care and will listen,
I still feel inadequate
in the face of such Grief.
Can I really help?
But God is calling
He is asking me to help my brothers and sisters;
in His name,
to humbly
listen and to care.
The first visits, so heart wrenching,
so tearful,
so lonely.
I feel like an inadequate intruder
with the Bereaved sharing
some of his deepest sorrows and
pains and
anguish and
regrets and
fears,
simply because
I am willing to listen,
and perhaps,
to care,

The preparation was right:

Don't counsel,
don't explain,
don't resolve,
don't lecture...
simply listen
and

care.

The visits continue,
the visited work through their Grief.
They talk more freely,
look more cheerful,
come to terms,
and... surprisingly,
welcome my visits;
They even wish to talk about me.
I do not know if
I have helped my friends to God's satisfaction;
but my friends in Grief
have touched my soul
by asking,
"Why has God been so good to them?"
and when greeting me
say,
"Hi, Brother John."
I joined to give,

but in return,
received much more.

Mobility

Chicago to Livonia to
West Bloomfield to Brussels, Belgium
to Orchard Lake

Orchard Lake
to Lancaster, PA
to Detroit to Sterling Heights, MI
to Chicago to Milford, MA
to Chicago to Troy to Clawson
to Grand Rapids to Chicago

Where does it end?
Where can we meet?
Where?

Lancaster to Scottsdale/Torch Lake
Sterling Heights
Milford, MA to Arizona
Clawson
Crystal Lake

Why can't Mobility work "To" as well as "From"

each other?

The Picture Window

Looking out at Torch Lake and Beyond
is truly God's Easel.

Through it,
moment by moment,
brushstroke by brushstroke,
He paints for me
an ever-changing world of beauty.

Each moment,
He presents for me a picture
which was never seen before and which
shall never be seen again.

I add each of them to my soul's collection

simply by stopping

and by seeing and by rejoicing.

Grief

I'm so embarrassed, so ashamed;
my Loved One died months ago and still,
I cry, I sorrow, I'm sad, I mope.
Something must be wrong with me;
others seem to recover so quickly,
but I can't.

The tears well up at any moment;
the sadness lingers;
anger weaves in and out.
Restful sleep eludes me;
dreams invade my mind;
my heart aches... and aches... and aches.

I keep wanting to tell people
how I *really* feel,
but few want to know;
most get tired of my repetition.
Something must be wrong with me.
Some friends even now seem to avoid me
as if my plight were contagious.

It's hard to pray;
I keep thinking of my Loved One,
of the moment of death.
But, in an instant,
My Lord gently sits me down on the grassy knoll
near the mount
and

He lovingly reminds me of
one of His invitations,
one of His eight lessons,
His call
TO MOURN.

He reminds me that my Loved One
is His Loved One
and that our relationship on earth
deserves a tribute
and that tribute is
My Mourning.

He reminds me that
my love for the One I lost
needs to be memorialized by me
which is best done by
Mourning.

My Lord
Blesses me for Mourning
and tells me that
it is only through *Mourning*
that I will be *Comforted*
and that the Comfort
will come from
God.

Love

Love is
Clearing a path for
The Divine which exists deep within me
To come in contact with, connect with, and
Ultimately unite with
The Divine which exists deep within you.

The Divine exists within each of us.

The path I clear,
(the addictions and idolatries I throw aside)
is, not only, within me,
but also in you
(your brokenness which I overlook).

The contact, the connection, the uniting
are made by the
very personal sharing of my feelings and
emotions,
by the sharing with you of myself,
with the gift of me to you.

I can love you
without your acceptance of my love
if you have not yet cleared a path to
The Divinity within you.
(I can overlook weaknesses you may not.)
(I can see the Divine within you, you may not.)

(You are lovable to me and
perhaps not yet to you.)

I can love you unconditionally
because the Love is
Christ's Love, God's Love,
which is eternal and unconditional.

In loving you,
I am energized
because
I complete the circuit of God's Love
allowing it to flow
from Him
to You
through me.

Love is
Connecting God, You, and Me
in His way.

Help

Dear God,
please help me to withdraw from:
illusion and pleasure,
worldly anxieties and desires,
works that You do not want and
glory that is only human display.

Please keep my mind free from confusion
in order that my liberty
may be always at the disposal of Your will.

Please help me to
entertain silence in my heart
to listen for Your voice and
cultivate intellectual freedom
from the images of created things
in order to receive the secret contact of Your
obscure Love.
Please help me to
Love all people as myself and
rest in humility and
find peace in withdrawal from
conflict and competition.
Please help me to
turn aside from controversy and put away
heavy loads of
judgment, censorship, criticism and the whole
burden of opinions that
I have no obligation to carry.

Please help me to
have a will that is always ready
to fold back within itself and
draw all the powers of the soul
down from its deepest center to
rest in silent expectancy for Your coming,
poised in tranquil and effortless concentration
upon the point of my dependence on You.

Please help me to
gather all that I am and
have all that I can possibly suffer or do or be,
Abandoning them all to You
in a resignation of a perfect Love and
blind faith and pure trust in You
to do Your will.

Then, Dear God,

Please help me to wait

in peace and emptiness and oblivion
of all things.

The Ever-Changing Past

If we are the sum total of
all of our past experiences,

Do those past experiences change
in relation to who we are Now
as we change
with each new experience?

If each experience in our life is simply like
the turning-over and putting in place
one of the pieces of
our Picture-Puzzle life,

Does each new piece change
in relation to the total picture
which grows
with each new puzzle piece,
with each new experience?

Perhaps,
The Past is not canned,
static, complete, finished, over?

Perhaps,
Our Past is fluid, Ever Changing,
more so even than
The Future,
which does not exist,

or The Present,
which simply is.

Maybe,
With each new experience in life,
We need to go back and re-examine the past
to see how it has changed.
(in relation to the New Now)
and

learn what New Lesson it holds.

Return

Left Northern Michigan last October.
Autumn's gala was nearly finished with
Its brilliant colors
succumbing to Winter's grays.
Left Torch Lake
windy, rainy, and cold;
made it easier to leave.

New Mexico en route South in November was
powerful;
Arizona thru April was
Busy;
Utah returning North in May was
Breathtaking;
But Torch
seems Home.

Left in gray;
Returned to gray.
Seemed to miss very little of Spring, although
the Daffodils stand proud and
Trillium bloom everywhere.
Some of the trees are showing green,
others are starting to bud;
the Evergreen
stand tall with evident new growth.
The uncut grass is high and green and moist.

Signs of New Life,
Signs of ReBirth
abound.

Awoke at 4 AM
this morning;
knew not why.
Went downstairs and
I saw why;
An old friend
came to visit and
bid Welcome
Home.

The rain had passed;
Torch was calm and
the sky was clear.
The Chateau in and out
was brightly lit
by Sister Moon
full and shiny
beaming with joy
at my return.

Welcome back North, John,
Welcome to Torch
Welcome Home.

Climbing the Mountain

We each and all begin climbing
The Mountain of Life
Starting from different positions.

And even when we take a path similar to
One before or after us,
We take it at different times, in different
seasons,
Under different conditions.

Also, some of us decide to learn from the
journeys of
Those who went before us,
While others decide to ignore others' successes
and falls,
and to blaze anew.

On the way up,
Our paths cross one another and
For a portion of the journey,
we may travel with others,
But finally we each must
Make our own way up.
Many struggle on the way up and tire;
Many stop to rest and
Decide to build their
Cabins, castles, palaces, cottages,
even churches
Rather than continuing on.

Family, career, success, control, possessions,
even religion and
Many other addictions
provide apparent Respite
from the tough uncertain climb.

Some decide to stop,
not to go on, Ever.

Trouble is no one can see through
The Cloud of the Unknowing which
Separates all the climbers from the Top;
We're climbing the Mountain of Life
Without being able to see the Top.
Some of our loved ones already have
Disappeared through it at their journey's end.

Climbing separately,
Crossing paths occasionally with another,
Urging each other onward,
Helping those stranded--who want help,
Encouraging those dissatisfied
with their self-made palaces,
To Go on,
We know we'll reach the Mesa of God on Top,
Where we'll no longer be alone,
But will indeed be joined by all
Who decided to Stay the Journey
All the Way to the Top.

It's our path and no one else's, but
It leads where everyone else's does--to unity

with each other
and
With God.

Renewal

Closeness to nature,
next to a lake or in the midst of a forest,
with no focus other than the internal
movements of the soul
has its own restorative qualities.

Nature is the Mother of Renewal.

Simply being near trees while in an aware state
can renew parts of a person's life.

When the distractions are minimized
and the feelings and emotional life
are maximized,
the sense of immediate mystery in the natural
world becomes visible
and palpable again.

We begin to feel nature
as the mother that holds one's ideas,
one's exclamations,
and one's outpouring of emotions
with utter sympathy.

By dwelling soulfully in a place,
a person can become reoriented to his center.

Pieces of one's self
that have been lost or missing
or stunned into silence,
can return,
either through finding some acceptance in the
grounds of nature,
or through stirring some memories in the
grounds of the psyche.

Wholeness can be found
through this combination of the wonder and
complexity of nature
brought together with
the surprising fountains of memory and
inspiration within.

It takes effort, timing, and grace
for those things to come together.

But those moments become
the swelling of the soul
that allows a person to return to regular life
with a renewed sense of self,
a renewed purpose,
and a renewed appreciation for
family, spouse, and loved ones.

Life's An Interstate

I merge into Life's Superhighway
starting out in the slow lane,
sometimes using the middle,
and occasionally running the fast lane.
No matter,
We're all headed to the same place.

Some stop along the way
for nourishment, refueling, even sightseeing.
Others have problems along the way,
malfunctions, flat tires, even accidents.
No matter,
they eventually get back into the journey.

Moving along,
I get upset when someone cuts me off,
moves ahead of where I think I should be.
I get impatient when someone
is going slower than I like.
I think all should be traveling
at my pace.
It doesn't happen that way.

Some get stopped along the way
for breaking the law,
for traveling life's highway too fast,
for causing others accidents and hardships,
for traveling recklessly.

Occasionally, some stop to help the stranded.
Many ignore the helpless.
People are fearful of hitch hikers.
Some vehicles are poorly maintained
and others are very old.
New cars look nice and perform well,
but their destination's the same.

Life's Interstate
ends suddenly... unexpectedly... without
warning.
It simply ends with
all the travelers entering free-fall,
thinking,

Why didn't we take the scenic slower

back roads?

The Blessing of the Trees

Cloudy, but not dark,

Autumn's Oranges, Reds, Yellows, Crimsons,
and Golds
replace the Sun's glow today.

Showery, but not cold,

The South Wind Warms all of us and
the Rain is a "She" Rain:
Soft and Gentle.

Biking up East Torch Lake Drive,
Surrounding Trees Dance to a
Gust of Wind
and
Anoint me with a Shower of Leaves
so thick
I can hardly see in front of me.

The leaves of all colors,
soft and warm
stick to me, cover me,
my arms, my legs, my chest, my face,
my bicycle.

I bike on,

the Gust calms,
the Trees rest,

the Leaf Shower clears,

the Leaves slowly slip off me,

but I feel
a part of Creation,

Confirmed so by

The Blessing of the Trees.

Church

Is the path
only for the guiltless?
Is the church only for
the sinless?

Can't be.
His Son showed Compassion
for the worst,
sided with the sinful,
the ostracized,
against the self-righteous,
the "saved."

The journey must be full
of setbacks,
of slips and falls.
Even His closest twelve
suffered abuse,
rejection, imprisonment.

Who promised
clear sailing, anyway?
Not He.

I know He Forgives,
even the worst I have done;
God knows,
I am sorry.
But why can't others forgive?

But does it matter?
Even His Godly Compassion
was looked on with scorn
by others.

Or is the lack of human forgiveness
part of the punishment,
part of the journey,
a stepping stone,
a test?

A test to
see how strong is my Faith,
a test to see if I still crave
human acceptance,
accolades,
human forgiveness?

His Love, His Compassion, His Forgiveness,

Who really needs more?

New Life

Eyes open,
sleep ended,
everything seems ok;
A new day, a new life.

Look around.
Everything seems ok;
the night rain has quenched a thirst,
the trees seem greener--happier,
the freshly planted grass fuzz
seems thicker, taller.
The birds fly by,
the lake ripples North
at South Wind's warm gentle urging.
Indeed a new day, a new life.

A new chance to see Creation,
a fresh chance to appreciate its beauty.
A new chance to Live,
and be loved if not by humans,
then by Mother Earth,
and the Creator, Himself,
in giving me a new day,
a new life,
another chance.

Rights

Throughout history,
males have been waging war over "rights,"
and to little avail.
Females have been the bastions of "Love."

and

It is Love that conquers all,
It is Love that survives in the end,
It is Love that brings us to God.

Jesus died on the cross
out of Love.
He chose not to wage war over His rights.
He died unjustly
For us
out of Love.

Unfortunately,
many of today's American females,
in their quest to be
"equal" to men.
have chosen also to battle over "rights"

abandoning
the far nobler
and vastly superior
Championship of Love.

In hopes that more of us will freely choose to
Love

and when faced with
having to choose
between Loving and "fighting" for rights,

choose Love.

We Pray.

Why Battle

Choice?

Of course we have the ability to choose.
Without free will to choose,
good deeds have no merit and
evil acts no culpability.

But the "right" to choose
comes not from Washington, nor
any government, but
indeed, from God.

God has given us free will.

Choose evil rather than good?
Yes, with free will,
one can choose evil rather than good.

Is the taking of an *innocent* human life
evil?
I believe so.
I believe that only God can do so.
I believe that choosing to
directly take the life of a baby
is evil,
is wrong.

No one's right to choose
should be lost;
but neither are all choices good.

The right to choose
does not make all choices good.

I am Pro-Choice of Pro-Life.

Bloom Where You Are Planted

Our plant has survived the climates,
the geographies,
the treatments to which we have subjected it.

It has overcome
some missed feedings,
occasional lack of attention,
and uprootings.

It has grown...
...matured, blossomed and bloomed
wherever we planted it.

It's offshoots have been planted elsewhere...
...and have grown and thrived on their own.

Our Plant, with our care and feeding...
...has bloomed wherever it has been planted.

Time to uproot and transplant again...
...But can it survive another move?

It's roots have gone so deep this time...
...friends, neighbors, church,
professional associates,
volunteer organizations, biking buddies,
golf mates...

And the roots go deeper each passing day...
...faster, it seems..

Better uproot quickly!

Time to replant...
...but where?
Try here and then there, if not,
then where?

Can our loving, mature plant...
...survive yet another move, at this stage in life?

Yes, it is strong...
...Our years of Loving Care and Nurture have
grown a lovely plant,

But it's roots are now deeper than ever...
...and don't seem to want to be pulled away
from this good fertile soil...

Need to ask the Master Horticulturalist...

...for guidance, O Lord.

Reflections

She looked into the windless lake,
saw her clear reflection,
and thought it was she.

Then the wind,
beyond her control,
came and sent ripples across the lake,
changing her reflection,
and she could no longer see herself
in the lake.

All her life,
her house, her children, her husband,
were a reflection of her,
and she thought it was she.
But the winds of life,
beyond her control,
came and changed them,
and they no longer reflected her,
and she could not clearly see herself in them.

And she discovered that
her real self could not be held in a reflection,
but only deep within herself.

Sister Moons

Tonight on Torch,
Shining Moon saw her Sister.
The windless lake,
rippling only slightly,
as if with awe,
gave us the chance
to see two moons,
sisters rarely seen.
With grace and beauty
they lit up the ink black sky
and turned the lake into a
shimmering mirror.

With joy
the sister moons moved closer and closer to
each other
wanting to meet, to kiss, to unite.
As they reached the horizon,
Torch Moon seemed to dissolve into her sister,
while Sky Moon blushed with happiness.
As Shining Moon set,
she emitted a brilliant orange color,
which shone upon the Lake
where her sister
once lived only moments before.

Music

Wind
pushing the water
up on to the shore.

Rocks
boldly protecting the shoreline,
standing firm
against the onrushing waves.

Water
slapping against the rocks
foaming as it encircles
the rocks.

Music
as wind, water, rocks,
join in celebration
of each other
and creation.

Rough sharp jagged rocks
worn smooth
over time
by wind, water
and the music
of Torch.

Paul

Many praised me
for protecting the Law and Tradition
by searching out those
who would divide the people
by their belief in He
who claimed to be Messiah.
The Praise made the effort seem worthwhile.

The Blaze of Light filled the countryside
and felled me to the ground.
I was paralyzed and confused.
I opened my eyes - to darkness!
I could not see!

Thus, I began my journey
to an inner vision of a profound reality.
I was stripped of my self-sufficiency and forced
to depend on others,
to enter a new form of relationship with them.
I was no longer Proud, Capable, Sure.

I was intelligent and well-educated,
but it was not by brilliant reasoning that
brought me to grasp the truth
that Jesus is the Eternal Expression
of the Living God.
It was the overwhelming experience of God,
first through Inner Revelation and then through
the Community of Believers.

My Faith was actualized both by the
Voice of the Spirit within me and by His
reaching me through others.
There is no separation in these realities.
I became so united
with the Word of God within me
that all of my actions were enclosed in the
One Circle of Light.

I was at first terrified but then
what I was given in Christ
made all the former power, adulation, security
and respect
seem like rubbish.

I had been immersed in the role of one who
upholds the law and tradition
and thus forgot my true identity.
When forced to be dependent on those who I
was persecuting
I had no choice but to be myself.
Only then was I able to
stop projecting my own pride
and self-righteousness onto others.

And once they got to know the true me
they trusted me and
their attitude toward me changed
because my attitude had changed.
As I got to know and accept my true self,
I was able to be honest with all whom I met.

I learned that

Christ is in God and

I am in God and God is in me.

Petoskey Stones

Treasure spawned by the sea

over millions of years

thrust into the earth and

pushing their way ever upward

seeking recognition and

a place of honor

through the keen eye and

in the loving heart

of a beautiful angel,

Catherine

Weed

Started out as a scraggly little weed
sprouting up in the front grass.
Looked like it really wanted to survive and
grow;
but it was, by most standards, ugly.
Decided to cut around it, let it grow,
see what it became.

Grow it did,
becoming a sharp pointy prickly Thistle.
Visitors laughed to see John
growing weeds in his front yard,
some thinking him somewhat kooky.
Knee-high, waste-high, chin-high,
through the summer it grew and grew
and grew.
Great Grandpa said it'd have blossoms,
Purple blossoms.
By Autumn when the visitors had left
and most everything else was fading,
the Mighty Thistle was taller then most people
bursting forth
with beautiful deep purple blossoms.

...even ugly appearing new-born can bloom
and give praise to God
if nurtured and allowed to grow.

The "O" "O" Approach

There is no lack of spiritual guidance in life,
only a lack of the awareness of
the guidance being given...

In attempt to fix a leaking toilet,
It was obvious that
a water seal needed to be "pushed" down
to stop the leaking.
Pushing, pushing, pushing
did not stop the leaking.
Inadvertently, so it seemed,
I "pulled" up on the seal;
the leak stopped.

Opposite Obvious

Pushing, Arguing, Fighting,
to get my way - by consensus,
with little success,
I concluded I'd be better off
"Giving In" for now,
trying to win another time.
In attempt to yield, to give in,
I was told
since I obviously felt so strongly about the issue,
I should have my way - without delay.

Opposite Obvious

Next time
try as I may without success,
I'll use

The **Opposite Obvious** Approach.

God is guiding us every moment of the day.

We only need to let go.

I Hear Not Your Attacks:

I cannot be attacked.
My ego can,
My body can,
but
I cannot be attacked.

It is not the Holy Spirit in You that is attacking.
It is your ego,
but not You.

If I perceive an attack from You,
it is a weakness in me,
not You.

It is my ego perceiving an attack on it.

I cannot be attacked

I hear not Your attacks.

Letting Go

He may have given me
the single moment of greatest joy in my life,
that special moment
when my heart leaped to the heavens,
that moment that will last to eternity,
that moment when I first saw
my first born
son.

That was only moments ago;
things change quickly.
Now he doesn't want to know me.

Poor Boy,
born to young shits,
who didn't know anything about life,
let alone raising kids.

Livonia,
Almost to Brazil,
then St. Nicks till Michigan,
St. Hugo,
then Brussels and St. Johns,
back to the USA alone
John Carroll,
all great experiences,
or were they?

First born,
set an example for the others?
be as successful as Dad?
live up to whose expectations?

Thirty-four
and suffering.

Embarrassment? Fear?
Guilt? Shock? Despair?

Don't know.

Won't share.
Can't help.
Won't share.

It's His Life.

Won't share.

Time to let go.

He'll find his way.
I did.

Come On In

I'd been sitting along the flowing stream for a long time. Many seasons had passed and life had been good to me. The views had been great when I'd really taken time to look and to see. Creation was truly beautiful.

I'd had plenty to eat and drink, yet I was thirsty. The water in the stream seemed so inviting, fresh, cool, and clear. What I ate and drank was good, but I wasn't satisfied, quenched. I'd traveled a lot up and down along the stream, but it came from places I knew not where and went to places, God knows where.

The funny thing about the stream is that it's close enough to see and hear but too far down to reach and scoop up a cupful. And the bank is so steep that I can't climb down and just get my feet wet. It seems that one just has to jump in to experience it. The trouble is that it's a very fast flowing stream--with plenty of rapids--and it's really not clear how deep it is or where it goes. And there's no evidence of a place to stop and climb out once I'd jump in. What to do?

It's pretty nice where I am and I can see the stream, but still I thirst for a taste. (Pepsi and wine and beer and booze and power and success and control and "things" just don't seem to quench my thirst.) Dare I risk them all and jump in? Skinny dip, leaving all behind (no pun intended)? It'll take a lot of Faith (to jump) and Hope (to keep going). And where does it end? or does it end?

I guess my bystander days are finished. I feel it's time to jump, to let go, to go where it takes me, to ride the rapids, see new sights, view all the people sitting along the banks (yelling for others to join me, "C'mon in, the water's fine"). I'll have to leave all my "things" behind, but so what. What good are they anyway, it's hard to use a nice car or stereo or computer riding the current anyway.

I wish I could take my loved ones with me, but I know that has to be their choice, not mine. And I dare not pull them in with me--they might drown. And hanging on to each other flowing down stream doesn't work anyway. Guess I'll have to leave all behind--relationships, too. If they decide to jump, I've got a hunch we'll all end up together somewhere anyway.

Hell with it, I'm jumping in.

Splash!

Wow, it is deep, can't touch bottom. And is it ever movin'! Look at all those bystanders gawking, trying to throw me a lifesaver (I'd like to throw them one). Some are really concerned about me, but the stream quickly takes me out of their range. Quite a few people in here with me--more than I saw from the shore. "Hi! How're you doin'? It's great, isn't it? When did you jump? Took some courage, eh?

The water tastes great. But it's funny, as good as it tastes and as satisfying as it is, my thirst is not yet quenched. In fact, I thirst even more. (I'll bet the more satisfying water is downstream.) But, hey, this no-attachment feeling is a little bit of ok. I'm now going with the flow, seeing creation from the right perspective, don't know where I'm headed, but somehow, it's not important. For some reason, I'm really glad I jettisoned everything and jumped in.

There is no end to this story or if there is, I sure don't know what it is...

The Call

In my search for identity
I tended to make my projects
absolute.
I tended to see others
as stepping stones
to achieve my projects.
In essence,
I made my projects
"ultimate";
I idolatrized them.

All around me in creation
is God's call
to grow.
His call is through
all the others around me.
By opening up
to His others,
I dis-idolatrize my own project,
make it relative,
die to myself a bit,
and grow.

I don't know where opening up to others leads

I tend to want to rest on any new plateau,
to make my new project
absolute and ultimate;
but there is more other,

more Gift,
out there calling me
to keep on growing.

Sin must be
consciously choosing my project, my idolatry,
rather than his Gift of Other,
His Gift of Growth.

But it's so painful:
I must die to my old project (myself) and
I must stretch
to the needs of the Others
He constantly gives me.

It's OK;
He showed me the way;
In the battle between Idolatry/Self/Project and
Suffering
Christ sided with Suffering.

God's Flashlight

Perhaps, I can be God's flashlight...

The energy source,
a touch of the Divine,
is within me.

I can't turn myself on,
but can be switched on
by the hand of God.

I can light the way for others,
with the Hand of God
pointing my way.

I can help others,
not by providing instructions,
or creating something new,
but simply by
providing guidance
by helping others see
what's already there
around and in front of them.

It's not what I do that helps,
but simply the light from my life,
the light from my turned-on energy source
within.

I am rechargeable,
and, in fact,
I need periodic recharging.

I can be recharged by
getting plugged into the ultimate energy
source
through others - through connections
to the Power source.

I don't choose whom to help,
but let God's hand
point me in the right direction.

My light also provides
some warmth.

My light opens a path
through the darkness.

I am beautiful only as an instrument
of help and guidance.

I corrode and die with non-use.

Thirst

My thirst consumes me.

And the more I drink, the more I thirst.

Prayer seems to beget the need to pray,
Spiritual Connections,
the need to connect more,

Readings, leads to other readings,
Helping others in Grief,
the opportunity to help more,
Inspirations, guidance,
Sharing, the excitement of sharing even more.

Am I not supposed to simply relax
and meditate
and contemplate?

I do, but

Doing so just inflames my Thirst,
Increases my Zeal,
Excites me more,
Moves me On and On

To Help
To Pray,
To Read,
To Share,

To Act

with Compassion
and
Zeal.

"For what am I looking?"
I am asked.

I know what it's *Not*;

Not an arrival,
Not an accomplishment,
Not an acquisition,
Not an attachment.

Each new Taste of God
Multiplies my Yearning,
Increases my Desire,
Magnifies my Zeal,
Explodes my Craving,

Consumes me.

Indeed, He must also be Thirsting for me.

Climb Down

I knew He was around;
I could feel His presence.

Others must have also;
crowds were gathering.

No way can I approach Him;
my life has been a litany of faults, sins, failures.

Maybe, just a look, a glance;
I need to see Him.

I think I can climb the tree and
rise above the crowd, above the tumult.

It's a struggle to get high enough,
but if I do, I may be able to see Him.

It is more peaceful up here, quieter;
there's less of a hustle and hassle, here.

And there He is;
I can see Him, I see Him!

And He sees me, looks at me;
"John, come down from on high;
Descend, for this day I am with you
in your house."

I thought I had to rise up above the rest
to see Him,

and He tells me to "Descend";

to be with Him *in my own house!*

I come down quickly,

retreating to my own place;

where, indeed,

He is with me.

I am here only to be truly helpful.

I am here to represent Him Who sent me.

I do not have to worry about
what to say or
what to do,

because

He Who sent me will direct me.

I am content to be
whatever He wishes,

knowing

He goes there with me.

I will be healed
as I let Him teach me to heal.

The Sun

Isn't it curious that

we cannot look directly at that

by Whose Light

we see everything.

Now

The past is sweet,
with so many wonderful memories,
and some painful,
and not so sweet,
some things I'd do differently.

But, no matter;
the past does not exist.

Yet, if I dwell there,
either on the sweet,
or the painful,
I dwell in a time and place,
that does not exist.

> The future will be better,
> I've worked hard to make it so,
> I'm looking forward to it,
> It will be good.

> The future does not exist,
> yet.

> If I dwell there,
> upon all the possibilities,
> all the what ifs,
> I dwell in a time and place,
> that does not exist.

It seems so many of my thoughts
take me to
the Past and Future,
I have little time
to think of the present moment.

Yet, all that really exists is
NOW.

He has told me that
Everything I will ever need in life
is available to me
here and now.
Certainly, He is with me,
here and now.

And, in fact,
despite my thoughts,

taking me
into the Past
(which does not exist)

          or

                  into the Future
              (which does not exist),

      I
have always been,
am now,
and always will be,

in the
NOW.

The Past is important;
it has helped make me
all I am today.

But I can't live here;
It does not exist.
No one lives here,
certainly not God.
(He knows no past.)

The Future is important;
it is where I am going.

But I can't live here;
it does not exist.
No one lives here,
certainly not God.
(He knows no future.)

So, here I am.
Here He is.
All I'll ever need is here.

I really need
to spend more time with God in,
the only place that exists:

NOW.

Dear God,

I feel closer to You
than I have ever felt... at least,
since I was a kid.

After 55 years,
I've finally taken the time
to talk with you,
to partition off enough silent meditation,
to listen to you.

Through daily Mass,
the Rosary,
my morning prayer,
spiritual readings,
and thoughts of You each hour,
I'm beginning to learn.

In helping to heal,
in Your Name,
I am being healed,
by You.

By writing,
and drumming,
and sounding my flute,
by reading and sharing
I am more alive in the NOW,
than I've ever been...
at least since I was a kid.

In turning my life over to You,

You've, indeed, taken it over:

I'm called each day,

I'm able to touch and heal each day,

I hear You each day.

Love, John

Morning Prayer

Dear God,

Please give me the Courage
and the Strength

to do Your Will today.

Help me to Love,

Help me to Heal in Your Name,

Help me to Grow in Faith,

and

Help me to help others find You.

Amen.

(Funny thing,
each day this prayer is answered.)

Don't plug me in.

Let me go with dignity.

Unless you can connect me
back up to my mother,
Don't connect me up to any
heatless machine;

that's undignified.

Let me go with pride, joy,
a sense of fulfillment, and
most important of all,
with dignity as a Human.

Connect me up to a glorious computer
and you preserve, not me,
but the machine,
and in the process,
allow it to siphon and suck and drain
what I value most.

The cord was cut with Love;

don't

attach it in fear.

Like a Picture Puzzle

of a million pieces,

My life seems made up of
individual, yet related,
sometimes coincidental events.

I don't know
how all the pieces fit together;
But as I experience more of life,
I begin to see portions take shape, form, and
meaning.

As He turns over each piece, each moment,
and reveals it to me,
fitting it in place,
putting it into perspective;

I begin to see
how the many moments and events of my life
are, indeed, related,
are part of the total picture.

The apparent chaos of all the loose pieces
spread out in front of me
begins to dissipate
and I begin to sense an order to it all.

I now know that

My life is the making of a beautiful picture;

that no piece will be missing;

and that every one of the pieces
(light and dark)

is needed to complete it.

The Viking Way

Sky ablaze
with a fiery red/orange sunset.

Warm mild breezes
filling the sails.

Sounds:
water up against the sailboat,
gulls begging for a handout,
weeping.

Flaming arrows stalking the target pyre.
Sails aflame!

Wood on fire, crackling.

A burial with Honor.

The boat and body sink,
the flames go water black
just as the sun sinks
below the far horizon.

A day and a man are gone.

We enjoyed them both;
None to follow will be the same.

Riding the Winds

When sailing troubled waters,
avoid ports of call;
Have Trust, stay His course,
let your sails stand tall.

Steer by His stars,
Follow His chart,
the Joy's not arriving,
but following your heart.

The schooner that's you,
is best, not ashore,
but riding strong winds
then asking for more.

Sailing Through Life

Life is not a matter of arriving
or accomplishing.
Life is the traveling, the Sailing.
The speed at which I travel and
the tack I sail are only partly
the result of what I do.
(God's Winds provide my power.)

Often, the Winds of Life change.
(How or when is not up to me.)
And when they change I must change.

I can't do the same thing
if I expect to stay on course.

In life, I sail with Winds
from North and South,
in Rough Seas and Mild,
and when I hit Doldrums
I know it's God's way
of reminding me

He's in control

and a New Wind is coming.

A Winter
On
Torch Lake

Why

I winter Torch because I wish to live
deliberately, to front the essential facts of life,
and see if I cannot learn what it has to teach,
and not, when I come to die, discover that I
had not lived.

I do not wish to live what is not life—living is so
dear—nor do I wish any longer to practice
resignation, unless it is quite necessary.

I want to live *deep* and suck out all the marrow
of life, to live so steadfastly as to put to rout all
that is not life, to drive life into a corner and
reduce it to its simplest terms, and if it proves to
be tough, why then to live the whole and
genuine toughness of it, and publish its
toughness to the world; or if it is sublime, to
know it by experience, and be able to give a
true account of it on the next stage of my
journey.

For most men, it appears to me, are in a
strange uncertainty about life.

(Paraphrased from Thoreau)

Winter on Torch

Why this driving need
to spend Winter on Torch—alone?

What little time I've spent in contemplation,
in meditation, has been wonderful.
I need more.
I need extended time and space in silence
to hear my God,
To better know Him—and me,
to let the artist in me emerge,
to pray.

Since buying the Chateau,
I've wanted to spend a Winter here,
Having tasted mostly Spring, Summer,
and some Fall.

Winter is an important part of the Chateau,
which I no longer wish to leave untasted.

In all my life,
Grammar school, high school, college, married
life…I've never lived alone.
It's time.

God is speaking, I need to listen.

To read, to write, to paint,
To play the flute and beat the drum
To walk, to ski, to meditate,
To be
Alone with creation;
This I feel compelled to do.

Where is the journey going to take me?
I do not know.
But, I will trust in God.

I trust that I will gain the courage and the
strength
to do His Will,
to heal in His Name,
to grow in faith
and to help others find Him.

Trails

I've blazed my trails
in the snow.

I ski on them often
in order to maintain them,
to keep them groomed,
to keep them packed and shining
so I can glide over them.

They are my trails
through the snow;
I made them and
I maintain them.

But each day,
the snow falls,
the wind blows
my trails fade,
are overrun by new snow,
and slowly disappear.

I must travel them
every day
and even then,
it's a battle
to keep them mine.

Old Man Winter laughs at me.

He allows me to have trails when he wants;
and when he doesn't
he simply blows them away,
covers them
as if they never existed at all.

I guess trails are not meant to keep,
they're meant to be made,
to be traveled,
to be given to the Old Man,
to be forgotten.

(One seldom looks back when
Cross-Country skiing, anyway).

Oh well,
better go make some new trails;

I guess that's really more fun anyway.

To Know Torch

To know Torch, one must live it.

To understand it, one must move around it.
To experience its moods, one must see it
at sunrise and sunset,
at noon and at midnight,
in sun and in rain,
in snow and in storm,
in summer and in winter
and in all other seasons.

To be one with Torch, one must sail it,
fish it, swim in it, even bathe in it.
Torch comes alive when one sings with it,
plays music to it, listens to it,
and shares secrets with it
around the sacred bonfire.

Spirits of many generations venerate Torch.
For those who get to know it truly
and share the veneration,
Torch becomes a passage to God.

Autumnal Torch

Temperatures cool,
Sunsets travel South,
Tourists leave,
Summer Cottages close,
Traffic eases,
Restaurants shut,
Boats are wrapped and stored.

Mother Earth,
as if breathing a sigh of relief,
at the passing throngs of Summer,
bursts forth with color.

Torch Lake,
relieved of its skiers and motorists,
spits out the docks and hoists and rafts
which marred its shorelines.

The deer,
less fearful of traffic,
wander freer.

The raccoons and squirrels and rabbits
seem to emerge from the woods
to reclaim their domain.

The birds,
never seeming to care if tourists come or go,
begin organizing for flights South.

Hunters
begin to ready for the shoot,
Skiers
anticipate the coming snows,
Locals
seem to go on with life
as if nothing were changing.

Leaves start to fall,
Spring's wildflowers,
long overcome by Summer's
give way to Fall's species.

Thick full clouds
are painted orange and red
by the setting sun.

Winds are cool and crisp and cold.
Torch's calms are surrounded by
dark strong waves.

Autumnal Torch proudly exhibits her
magnificence.

Blessed

The Sun
shone through the clouds
to form a brilliant circle of light
on the water across the lake.

As the clouds moved across the sky,
the circle of light came across that lake
towards me.

When it reached me,
the water shimmered and sparkled so brightly,
I had to close my eyes.

The sun
warmed my face and hands and
God said,
"John, you are indeed Blessed."

Indeed, I am.

Name of the Wind

Who's wind is this, anyway?

Just yesterday,
Autumn glorified in all her magnificent colors.

The Fall sun shown brilliantly
through the oranges, crimsons, golds, greens,
reds and yellows of
Mother's magnificent trees.

Miss Autumn gazed back at itself
in Torch's crystal mirror,
held still as all creation seemed to hold its
breath in awe.

But today...

the sun is nowhere to be seen,
hidden by dark ominous clouds,
moving quickly across the skies.

No reflections can be seen
in Torch's face
whipped into a white-capped frenzy.

And Autumn's brilliant colors
now being shed
lack luster in the wet cold air.
Lying on the ground,

they give little evidence
to yesterday's glory.

Who's wind is this, anyway?

Is it Autumn's
simply using its slang name?

Is it Winter's
telling us to beware, he's coming?

Is it Autumn's wind,
just tidying its house and letting us know that
we should have appreciated its
short-lived brilliance?

Is it Winter's wind
clearing the decks for its arrival and letting us
know that its time is not one of colors and
calm, but cold and chaos?

Perhaps it's neither;
simply the curtain between acts of
Mother Earth's Great Production.

The Season of the Long Dark

Night is so hungry,
it demands the sharing of our dinner
it partakes of our breakfast.
It yields only to lunch,
and then very reluctantly.

Darkness prevails;
it boasts its victory over daylight
not only by territorial conquest,
but also through its cloudy soldiers
who keep Sun's rays
imprisoned.

Darkness' victory is witnessed, not only, by
kingdoms retreating in hibernation
but also by humanity's somber moods
acknowledging surrender to the deep dark.

To conquer those
who would vainly fight Darkness
Night harkens cousin Winter
whose armies of snow and wind and ice
freeze humanity's somber moods
and cover the hibernating kingdoms.

Deep Dark Rules.

But its victory is shallow.

For in darkness and in winter's solitude
we can find contemplation,
we can find ourselves,
we can find God.

Darkness has been duped.

It's victory
merely a stepping stone
to the
Glory of Spring and New Life in God
to follow.

Escape

When we get out of the glass bottles of our
ego, and when we escape like squirrels turning
in the cages of our personality and get into the
forests again, we shall shiver with cold and
fright but things will happen to us so that we
don't know ourselves.

Cool, undying life will rush in, and passion will
make our bodies taut with power, we shall
stamp our feet with new power and old things
will fall down, we shall laugh, and institutions
will curl up like burnt paper.

                    D.H. Lawrence

Quest

And when I got off the treadmill going
nowhere, and when I let go of the control I
never had, nor would ever have, and I got into
the forests again, I shivered with cold and with
fright, but things happened to me so that I
didn't know myself.

Warm, Loving, God rushed in, and His passion
made me glow with heat, and I held my head
and hands up high and yelled,
"God *is* Love!"
I laughed with tears and the things I'd feared
curled up like burnt paper.

                    John Chuchman

God's Easel

My picture window,
looking out to Torch and beyond,
must be God's Easel.

Each and Every moment He paints on it for me
a new picture,
altering a shade here,
changing a hue there,
moving a cloud,
turning a wave,
adding a bird.

His sun brightens a tree,
casts a new shadow,
brings out a new color.

His skies run from deep blue to orange and red
at sunset. His water changes from blue and
green to aqua or even gray. His clouds, mostly
bright, He sometimes makes dark and ominous.
His trees and leaves, He gives a myriad of
colors. He sprinkles with rain, He coats with
snow.

He blends moments into hours into days, days
into weeks and months,
months into seasons and years,
but only moment by moment,
brush stroke by brush stroke,

some hardly perceptible.
He is pleased with all of His Creations,
never starting over,
simply changing,
brush stroke by brush stroke,
moment by moment.

Either God is in perpetual search of that
perfect painting or each is perfect and He is
simply letting me see them
moment by moment,
painting by painting.

All I need to do
Is take the time to look
And enjoy.

Crescent Moon

The waters calm,
the stars dim,
quiet prevails,
as the crescent moon
slowly sets
with great majesty.

Many cherish and adore the setting sun;
few see and appreciate the setting moon.

The sun sets with great glory and fanfare,
the moon with delicacy and grace and
mystery.

Once set,
the waters go dark,
the stars brighten,
darkness prevails
and night takes over its realm,
moments ago dominated by

crescent moon.

Enjoy it all.

Admire the blue skies;
bask in the sunshine..

Rebirth with Spring's buds;
marvel at the new growth.

Feel awe at Autumn's brilliant colors;
revel in the brilliance.

Enjoy the soft winter snow or
early spring rain.

All these get adulation and admiration,
but what of
those powerful dark days
everyone calls gloomy.

Who labeled these gemstones
dreary?

Who precluded appreciation of this aspect of
God's realm?

Thick, powerful, fast-paced clouds,
in sixty-four shades of gray,
rumbling, tumbling, twirling,
war-dancing overhead;

All of creation
holding its breath in awe,
trees bowing in the winds
to the mighty gray fists clenching the sun, ruling
the sky;
the water obediently moving wherever told,
animals still.

The reverent calm before and after,
made possible – and enriched – by
the beautiful noisy fury of
the thundering
Tempest, Turbulence, Turmoil, Tumult.

Run not, turn and face it, respect it,
revel in its Power.

Alone

Here I am,
all alone,
on the edge of humanity,
facing that Old Man,
Winter.

That first snowfall,
so calm, so gentle, so soft,
a lulling strategy no doubt.

Here I am, all alone,
houses on all sides vacant;
no one but me to face his cold, icy, blows.

Wind comes straight across the water,
whipping Torch into a white capped frenzy,
trees swaying, shaking, bowing;
the Old Man is starting to howl.

Here I am,
all alone on the edge,
no land to protect me from his wrath,
straight off the water he comes,
encircling the Chateau,
laughing.

That strip of land across Torch
disappears,
It's as if I'm at sea –
maybe I am – I hear the waves.
Here I am,
all alone to face his fury;
his icy breath finding their way
through Chateau's warps and wrinkles.

The snow he moves about at will,
creating mounds and drifts and valleys,
covering my shovelings and tracks,
encasing the shrubs in seasonal tombs.

Here I am, all alone, at the point;
I defend all those to the East and South,
I am humanity's hope,
I must stand tall with the Old Man,
I must suck him in, and breathe him out,
weather his challenge, nay
enjoy his fury.

Here I am, not alone at all,
just simply learning from creation,
that *I am* Old Man Winter and
what I am facing *is me* and
if what is good in me is to be reborn in Spring,
then, what is not, must die in this cold darkness
around me.

Mother Nature

tucks in her sleeping children,
making sure they're covered
with their new white blanket.

They sleep.

Father Winter,
double checking that
all is well,
switches on the moonlight,
sighs,
and glows with pride.

The Angels Bless,
decorating the frosty spread
with twinkling stars.

The countryside glitters.

God smiles.

Surprise

To wake each morning
and not know what awaits outside.

Has the Old Man
unloaded a mountain of snow
for me to shovel.
or has he simply
blown it around to cover my clear walkways.

Has he covered creation
in an icy case,
or melted some of his prior handiwork.

Did he hide the moon and sun-to-come
with his dark snow-laden clouds
or has he blown them away
so we can see the stars
and rising sun.

Is it calm and peaceful
or stormy.

What will the outside thermometer show,
zero or below,
fifteen, twenty;
or will he freeze my bones
with wind chill.

Just don't know,
each day an adventure,
all I can do
is arise,
look outside,
marvel
and

turn the coffee on.

Related

He and I
are much the same,
this Old Man Winter and me.

And not just because
white and gray seem to be
our favorite colors.

Trying hard to get attention
to gain respect,
sometimes by blowing hard,
sometimes by icing down.

Letting everyone know
we need no one,
and people better pay us heed,
for we can affect their plans.

Working hard to show
that despite our ferocity,
we can be beautiful;
that despite our noise,
we can be peaceful,
that despite our exterior harshness,
we are really soft and gentle.

Old Man Winter and I,
some despise us,
run away,
fear us,
but many have fun with us,
enjoy us,
especially the kids.

To many, we represent the end of life,
to others its wisdom,
for in our solitude and tranquility and darkness,
is self,
is God.

Yes, this old man and I are a lot alike,
respect us, fear us, enjoy us,
whatever;
we will both be gone in time
giving way to
Spring and new life.

But each of us
will have left our mark on creation,
and you will learn
that Winter is as truly loving as any,
maybe more.

Shoveling

The crisp cold air
feels so clean.
It fills your lungs
and seems to give new life.

The shovel glides
over the patio
pushing the soft dry snow ahead of it
leaving trails on both sides,
for return pushes.

A lift at the end of the patio
sends a misty white trail into the air
with the snow falling ahead with a very soft
thud.

You warm up with each pass
and your visible breath dissipating into the cold
air says
"I'm alive, indeed."

With each pass,
the patio looks better and better
retaining a white film
simply to remind you
it's winter.

The job is exhilarating,
the air is fresh,
the exercise is good,
the results of your effort are clear.

No matter that the job'll
have to be done again tomorrow and
fifty times more;
it's not the end product – a clean patio
that's fun;
It's the doing.

Besides, it's much more fun than keeping it
clean in the summer…

New Season

How marvelous!
Autumn exits, not
in the glory of all her magnificent color,
but with a gray, sad, dreary ending
to a grand season.

How well planned
by Mother Earth!
The leaves have been long gone,
the color spectacle forgotten,
the temperatures afar from summer.
Autumn has had its glory,
and now exits with class,
with style,
with a somber sad farewell.

And the Longest Night comes.

But the next morning,
Welcome Winter!

Mother Earth brings on the new season,
the move North,
the lengthening days,
with a magnificent brilliant snowfall.

All the gloom, and all the gray is gone,
replaced by the glisten and gleam of new
fallen snow.

The harsh damp end to fall
gives way to the soft sparkling of winter.

All of creation trying to stay low
in fall's final days,
seems to stand tall and proud
in new glorious glistening garments.
The harsh autumnal winds and rains
have been replaced by winter's soft and
majestic silence.

The new season enters in style and
leads us to wonder,
will the rest of its show be as tranquil
as the first act?

Alone

Alone? Are you kidding?

Surrounded by these beautiful, stately, loving
trees, sheltering me, protecting me, watching
over me.

With ducks still in Torch's water,
with rabbits ever-jumping about,
with families of turkeys marching around,
with deer always dashing here and there,
with birds who refused – like me –
to fly South,
with cats and dogs,
with moles and coons and possum
(or is it possi?),
with owls, and mice,

alone? Be serious.

With Old Man Winter putting on his best
production, Grandfather Wind whipping the
waves and painting the sky with clouds white,
and gray, and black.
With Old Sol
shining through at every chance and giving
that snow a sparkle and Sister Moon lighting it
up at night brighter than some days.

Alone?
Maybe in the city
isolated from all these friends,
but not here
in Mother Nature's showcase.

In this front row seat,
I'm not sure how many other people are
seeing, but even if there's no one else in
attendance in this amphitheater,

I'll sure enjoy the cast party
(the Director invited me)
because the performance is outstanding.

Can't imagine what they'll do
for an encore...

Keep 'em Guessing

Each day so different:

Yesterday, Bright Sun
No Winds,
Calm meandering Lake,
No sounds save the occasional winter bird or
popping tree,
Brilliant white Snow
Glistening in the Sunshine,
Peace and Majesty
to the Winter Sonata.

Today, its own day,
Howling frigid Winds,
Dark ominous sky,
Clouds laden with Snow rumbling overhead,
Snow dancing, whirling, drifting
Lake churning and splashing,
covered with whitecaps,
Darkness dabbed with grays of all shades,
Animals in hiding,
Whirlpools of snow dancing to the frenzied
notes of Winter Overture.

Don't take me for granted,
says the Old Man,
I've seen it all and will dish out more,
Yes, I can be beautiful but
I can be ferocious,

Sometimes calm, and often Violent.
Try and figure me out and I'll fool you,
for the Old Man of Winter
is not the Birth of Spring,
(although I sometimes break it
with my winds);
nor the Laziness of Summer,
(although my storms will
occasionally remind);
nor the Tranquility of Autumn,
(although my cold will herald);
Old Man Winter is his own Man:

Predictable,
only in his
Unpredictability.

Royalty

In Arizona,
Sun is King

He comes up most mornings
like
Thunder!

Sunshine Rules.

In the North Country
in Winter,

Daylight tiptoes in,
sneaks up on Night,
treads lightly on Darkness.

Sun
hopes the Old Man
will part the power clouds occasionally
so he can peep through.

Darkness rules here.
Night dominates now.
Blacks and Grays are the colors du jour.

Sunshine, although welcome,
like a tourist,
certainly is not a local,
not a full-time resident.

And even when
Sunshine is allowed in,
he must leave his warmth behind,
lest the Old Man's
Snowork suffer
or anyone dare think
Spring.

Occasional
sunshine, fine;
even Brilliant Sunshine,
but,
Absolutely no warming,
no sign of meltdown,
no indication of Spring,
Not now,
Not in the Kingdom
of
Dark Cold Night.

The Battle

The Battle Continues

Winter's army conquers
the lesser foes.

His winds and cold,
His clouds and snow
turn the weaker foe
from battling lakes
to captured imprisoned rinks of ice.

But Mighty Torch battles on.

The battalions of cold attack its flanks,
creating outposts of ice on the banks,
but Torch's waves quickly
overrun the enemy.

Winter's companies of snow
do little to overcome the lake,
as Torch takes on any and all comers,
as if they had not been.

The battles continues
day and night,
Winter sending in its troops
wave after wave after wave
of cold and wind and snow;
with Torch valiantly resisting,

flowing proudly in the winds,
North or South, West or East,
Colors brightly shining,
be it cold or sun,
slowing using its reserves of heat and
dreading the day

the enemy withdraws
its winds,
and sends alone
the proud mighty frigid battalions of cold.

Mighty Torch,
too proud and beautiful
to be captured and imprisoned,
without
a Valiant fight.

Fury

The Old Man's Fury

He's really showing his stuff, now.

Dark, ominous, sky;
strong icy cold winds
blowing the snow into
mounds and drifts,

Torch churned up by a
strong Northwest wind
whipped into a white capped frenzy.

Trees bending in self defense,
schools closing early,
road crews struggling
to keep roads open.

Autumn? Spring?
distant memories,
far off visions;
this is the Old Man's time;
He's in control.

The Old Man's
power and fury and might
being shown for all to see
and never forget;

Peace?
The only peace one can find today
is within;
outside there is no peace,
only noisy signs that
Old Man Winter
rules, indeed.

Family

It seems Relatively easy
feeling a part of nature,
a fellow member of creation
in Spring, when life begins anew
and all is abloom with new vibrancy,

or in Summer, with the Sun shining brightly
and all bask in Nature's glory,

or even in Autumn, with its myriad of colors
and soft mellow days.

It's much tougher
feeling a part of this Mother Earth, when Old
Man Winter
wreaks his havoc on creation.

For the night is long and
the day is not much brighter.
And his icy wind cuts to the bone
and keeps you inside by the fire so warm.
And he blows his snow around in fits and drifts
to make difficult if not impossible to move
about.
Yes, he breaks the silence but only with
whirling winds which are far from friendly.
Even Torch seems to deny brotherhood,
churning and beating on the shore, saying
"don't come near."

I know I am a member of this Old Man's family,
too;
I just don't know how
we're related.
I feel like an outcast, a stepson,
not really a part of this icy household.

I sense no love out there at all.

but maybe, just maybe,
he's trying to show me
Love's not really out there in any case;

It's within
and
Now's the time
to find it there.

Maybe this is the real season of love...

Perhaps it comes too easy in Spring, Summer,
and Autumn.

Sister Torch

Sister Torch, nonchalantly showing off
some of her magnificent blues
in the crisp fall sunshine...

Uncle Wind, with no place to ho in particular,
tickles her with puffs and breezes,
causing giggles and ripples, snickers and
swells...

Great Uncle Sun, not wanting to be left out of
the fun,
decorates Sis' blue
with buttons of sparkling, glimmering, glittering
gold...

And a good time was had by all
with the birds and angels and hardly anyone
else noticing
...except me.

But Great Uncle Sun left early, Uncle Wind
moved on,
Sister Torch stopped giggling and
I just sighed.

The Shortest Day

It may have been the bleakest,
gray and dreary,
until
the unseen sun set,
and

Grandfather Winter
decided to brighten things up
with a brand new coating
of soft, white, sparkly,
snow.

The grayness was gone, Winter was here,
and the days will now be brighter and longer.

No Wonder

No wonder they call you "Old Man" Winter

One minute, a peaceful, sweet, tranquil old
guy,
reminding us of bygone days
and lovely memories.
The next moment,
a cantankerous, shouting, trouble-making
fussbudget,
yelling and hollering,
and causing chaos.

We don't know whether
to love you or be angry at you.
You comfort us one moment,
then chill us to the bone the next.

But, life just wouldn't be the same without you,
"Old Timer."

Our folly:

trying to make a mark in the world,

a place in history,

a contribution to society,

leave a legacy...

trying to make ski trails
in the snow

that our grandkids can use

when we're gone...

Who wants to wear the white?

The landscape has no choice,

though it keeps shifting the mantle to and fro

into drifts and mounds and valleys.

The trees, beautifully bedecked in white,

shake it off while dancing in the winds,

knowing full well, there'll be another coating.

Torch, whose greens and blues glow in
contrast,
also dances with the blowing winds

and in the process

dawns its mighty winter whitecaps.

In the winter, white is in.

When asked,

"When did I devote my life to God?"

I thought it was a silly question
(But it wasn't because
it compelled me to think of the answer).

There was/is no point in time, no moment,
when I gave my life to God;
it was/is a continuous giving;

It's daily,
it's moment by moment,
constantly.

Valentine's Day,

I bought eight dozen--yes, eight dozen
flowers.
I took the bucket
(they gave 'em to me in a bucket o' water)
to Meadow Brook Nursing Home,
took off my hat and coat,
and made my way through the halls,
room to room, sweetheart to sweetheart.
To each I met,
in bed, in wheelchair, walking, sitting,
in the beauty parlor, in the cafeteria,
in the hall,
I gave a flower and asked,
"Would you be my Valentine?"
It was the most beautiful Valentine's Day
of my life;
For as each gal graciously accepted
my flower,
she smiled and her face lit up brilliantly and in it

I saw God.

Summer is so expansive

With summer's clear bright sunny days,

one can see for miles.

Winter, not;

It seems to bring the whole world in on one;

Everything seems so close.

Winter calls one inside

to find life within.

Battle

The Battle between North and South
continues...

The North Wind churns up those waves,
moves the deep black heavy clouds
overhead,
almost buckles the trees--at least the older
ones,
chills us to the bone.

Then the South Wind takes control,
the clouds disappear, the sun shines through,
Torch's whitecaps disappear, but not the
waves,
but she makes us feel warmer.

The Warrior
and
The Healer.

It's futile.

Try as you may to get through to us,
Great Sun,
It's futile.

I see your outline up there,
occasionally,
as the blowing snow clears.

I know you're trying to warm us,
but this is the Old Man's time,
Winter's glory;
and he decides how warm we'll be
and how much of you we'll see.

But, thanks for trying, and keep on shining,

I know you'll get through one day.

Respect

I met an ole timer
who had spent a lot of time
on Torch Lake.
His words of advice:

"Maintain a deep respect for Torch,
Do not fear her,
but keep a deep respect for her."

Only in Winter

Could Torch be more beautiful than it is in
Spring,
when all of Nature's newborn
splendidly decorate it?

Could Torch be more beautiful than it is in
Summer,
when Hot Bright Sun and Warm Winds
beckon us a loving welcome?

Could Torch be more beautiful than it is in
Autumn,
when it basks in the
Bursting Oranges, Reds, Crimsons and Golds?

...Only in the Winter,
when the Brilliant Sun and Blinding Bright White
Snow
contrast Torch's Blues and Torch's Greens into a
Colorama
seen in no other season of the year.

Trees

Spring; They Blossom

Summer; They Bloom

Autumn; They Burst with Color.

And so that they don't miss out,

Old Man Winter
takes his paintbrush

and lines them
with a Beautiful Soft White Mantle.

Trees; made for all seasons.

Grey

Winter's gray dominates the morning,
the countryside covered with a deep white
snow,
and temperatures proudly around zero.

Torch refusing to succumb,
steams with defiance at winters charges.

South Wind blows strongly
with the night storm's passing.

Torch's steam,
angers the Old Man,
who blows it away
and sends it North.

East Wind

Torch confuses with an East Wind.

It knows the South
with its warm true winds.

It is intimate with the North
dawning its whitecaps in respect.

It loves the West off the Big Lake,
allowing sailors a tackless trip up and down.

But this Easter...
Calms, whirlpools, a bit of Norther,
A feel of Souther,
...confusion.

Puzzle

Like pieces of a puzzle,

The Old Man constantly shifts and moves
the pieces of ice
around Torch's shoreline

gradually finding the right spot for each,
fitting them in place,
squeezing them in tight,
making the ice picture solid and firm,
constantly adding another and another,
shifting, fitting,
squeezing, freezing.

The Old Man's havin' fun...

Letting Go

Letting Go of everything

and jumping into the depths of my soul,

I come out,

not in some deep dark cavernous place,

but instead,

among beautiful, sharing, helpful, loving
friends.

(Were they there all the time?)

Living with Joy

Invite her in
and your whole life will change.
She'll force some of your comfortable old
cronies out.
Fear, Anger, Cynicism, Anxiety
all will have to leave.
Worry won't live in the same town,
let alone your pad.
Pessimism won't come near you anymore.
The other challenge you'll face is
Joy likes parties;
the word will quickly spread
that you're with Joy,
and everyone'll want to be with you—
loneliness will split.
And some great new friends will show up
at your place:
Laughter, Optimism, Happiness, Peace, Humor,
Trust.

So if you decide to live with Joy,
be prepared for a radical change in lifestyle.

But don't worry (it's not forever),
if it doesn't work out,

you can always go back to being sad.

Rescue

Funny,

just as the Old Man tightens
his cold icy grip on the Northern countryside,

the Great Sun
is seen moving North,
as if, to the rescue.

Just as Torch gives up the battle
and goes "underground"

The Great Giver of Light and Heat
shows the frozen North,
that it is returning.

In hopeful preparation,
days begin reclaiming lost time

from the darkness.

Islands

Islands of Water
in a sea of Ice.

Overnight,
the ice has reached out halfway across Torch
leaving in its wake
islands of water.

Gone is the noisy din
of frigid waves banging against the shore;

Winter pulls back some of its mighty forces
and lets the ice,
now in complete control,
smother powerful Torch into submission,
with the steaming pools providing the last gasp
of seasons past.

Ice

The ice has gained a foothold
on Torch's shoreline.

It grows minute by minute
expanding on into the Lake.

Torch's waves attempt to beat at it
to break it up
to stop it from growing,
but no more.

Now the ice is strong enough
to eat the waves,
push them down under it,
keep its foothold secure.

Attack

Winter's troops are making their move
against Torch.

Surrounded by the snowy shore,
Torch is now being invaded
all along its shoreline
by the advancing Ice Brigade.

Torch sends its mighty waves
to break up the ever-growing ice,
but Winter's temperatures
bring in more and more
invading bergs.

Winter's attack has begun.

More Ice

Ice all the way out to the drop off!

Twisting, whirling, beating
winds shipping up the snow.

Winter's full blown attack is underway.

Torch
seems battered and beaten
ready to succumb,
the frigid, below-zero temperatures
slowing all her attempts
to break up the ice
and beat back Winter's charge.

...and yet, she steams in rebellion...

Snohara

Torch is a lake, no more.

It is a desert of white cold sand,
blown into ever shifting snodunes.

Whirlwinds of white touch the ice sporadically,
or at least so it appears.

I could walk across the less-than-two miles,
but dare not,
for fear of the Old Man's breath,
and the penalty for desecrating
Angry Torch forced to go underground

for now.

The Last Artery

The last artery
flowing up the very center of Torch,
is now hardening.

It is surrounded by a sea of hard white,
portions smooth
where Winter's Wind has blown it so;
portions rough and jagged,
giving evidence to Torch's battle against the
freeze.

Winter's massive forces
have been withdrawn, no longer needed;

Even the sun is welcome;
All the Old Man uses to finish off the job,

is cold.

Love Affair

Whipped by cold winds,
filled with snow,
slowed by sub-zero temperatures,
Torch was surrounded by enemy ice,
who encroached on her from all shores.
When it looked like
she would succumb to the Old Man,
an old old friend,
South Wind,
comes and gives her hope,
at least for some more days free.
They kiss
and together
push back and even melt some of the enemy
with their love affair
which outlasts
all seasons,
all the years,
many winters.
Even if Torch is finally stilled,
South Wind
will remain a sweet loyal lover.

Friend

I know a tree

He's been around a long time,
longer than I.

He's an evergreen
and He is, indeed, ever green.

In the Summer,
He provides us with needed shade.

In the Fall,
He proudly displays his royal dark green
amongst the myriad of fall colors.

In the Winter,
He shelters the Chateau
from the Old Man's cold and icy winds.

When I play my drum, He dances in the Winter
winds.

When I play my flute, He sways with the
melody.

And when I talk, He listens.

He is tall and stately, yet somehow gentle and
soft.

He has seen many things, and will share his
knowledge,
if we listen.

He has powerful energy, and will share his
power,
if we pray.

He teaches, that despite many years, one must
stay flexible and soft,
and accept change
for the aged who become rigid and hard and
inflexible, break and die.

My friend the Tree, continues to change, and
in the Spring,
will grow anew,
and I will watch Him

and marvel.

I treasure
my friend,
the Tree.

Old Man

Even the old man can't stay
furious all the time.
He rants, raves, ravages,
huffs, puffs, blows,
bends the trees,
freezes the water,
chases the people,
just to prove
He's in control.

But he can't keep it up all the time.

And when he rests,
all of creation breathes a sigh
of relief.

The trees,
although bedecked in white,
stand tall and still.
The walkways and driveways
are cleared and shoveled.
The snow is quiet,
the wind is calm.

And then the moon
takes control of the sky
and lights up the world
for all to see.
Animals scamper,

humans peak out
or even walk or ski about,
and
the whole countryside
is lit up.

And although it's a glorious moment,
there is no shouting,
for it's a calm, proud, sweet, glory.
All seems still
as if to say to the Old Man,
We heard you, we felt your icy winds,
we were blinded by your
blowing snow,
but that is past,
and now, this night,
the moon has shown us your real work of art,

A silent night,

a holy night,

when all is calm

and all is bright.

Light

Even though the light
is not hers in the making,

She lights up
all the heavens
and all of God's creation.

The stars so brilliant
when she's not around,
disappear
in her brilliance;
only a few dare
peek out during her
illumination.

The cold icy earth,
is not made to feel any warmer
--it may even feel colder--
glows in her glory.

Torch, finally succumbing
to Winter's wrath,
his incessant onslaught
of snow and wind and cold,
bears her new hard brilliant crust.

That shining pathway across the lake
from me to the moon,
most of the year non-walkable,

could now be followed
on foot or ski,
as if to say
I can now traverse the pathway to heaven.

The snow, trees, rooftops,
everything is aglow in the
Moon's brilliance.

(I, indeed, can outshine the stars
by simply allowing
God's light to radiate upon me
mirroring it to others,
who then also
will glow in His brilliance.
If that piece of cheese or rock or ice in the sky
can do it,
surely I, His child, can.)

Lessons from the Great Tree
on the Night of the Full Moon

If only I could learn to be like the Great Tree
I see in front of me.

It does not control, nor try to control,
events around it;
it simply stands tall witnessing them all.
It weathers all seasons, hot and cold,
wet and dry;
using each to help its growth.

It bends a little in storms,
so as not to break;
but after they pass--and they all do—
it stands tall.

It wears the ice and snow of harsh seasons
with beauty and pride;
it uses the summer suns to grow,
while giving shade to all who want it.

It stays true to its color,
while others may change;
it grows slowly, but steadily.

The Great Tree is wise beyond measure,
controlling and trying to control
only itself,
only the way it reacts to the events of life.

It is calm, quiet, strong, yet gentle;
It provides shelter for those who want,
and food for those who need.

The Great Tree,
so beautiful in its splendor,
so strong in its steadfastness,
so eloquent in its silence,
so serious in its work, yet

always finding time to laugh and dance
with the winds.

If only I could learn to be
like the Great Tree
I see in front of me.

Awe

The morning moon,
not yet hidden by the rising sun,
honors me.

It looks down,
nearly full,
and bathes the earth
in its soft glowing light.

No wind,
silent calm,
The Great Tree
casts a magnificent shadow
on the silvery crusted snow.

The windblown
snow dunes
on icy Torch
take on an eerie cast.

Stars, hiding
in deference to
the reigning moon,
are nowhere to be seen.

The nighttime is transformed;
darkness no longer prevails,
the moonlight has
overcome the night

even before the dawn.

Swiftly moving clouds
seem to swirl around her,
providing a crown, a halo,
a mystical aura.

As they pass, the intensity of light
varies moment by moment
creating a constantly changing
mystical landscape.

The flute plays,
my drum beats,
in honor, in thanks, in awe,
of
the Blessing
to be a part of
His Beautiful Creation
now.

Ice Fishermen

Just like the ice-fishermen,
poking through Torch's icy crust
to reach within her depths
to gain some treasures,
some food of life;

I am a fisherman
poking through the crust of everyday life,
to go deep within
and also gain treasures,
spiritual food, the voice of God.

We both discover
the sustenance below.

Glory

In his glory,
he is.

He is so proud,
having conquered Torch,
even earlier than normal,
having set records
for cold
and for snow,
he even lets the Sun shine,
and brilliantly no less.
But with his icy blowing winds,
no one spends any basking time outdoors
and
even die-hard Northerners
are crying uncle,
saying, "enough already,"
and thinking Spring
(or trying to).
This is his time;
he can chill you to the bone in an instant,
close off your visibility in a moment,
slide you on ice and trap you in snow;
if he wants you, he can have you.
This is the Old Man's time
and he's Proud of it,

just ask him.

The Black Hole

There is this black hole
deep within us.

It is a deep silent swirling whirlpool;
trying to suck us and everything around us
into it.

All our lives we learn to fight this black hole,
to resist being sucked under.
We grab onto anything and everything we
can
in the outside world
to help us from being sucked down into
the black hole within us.

We resist because
we don't know where it leads,
where it would take us,
what would happen to us.

We fight to stay
where we are,
to face what we think we know,
to stay outside
the black hole deep within us.

It keeps swirling,
silently sucking, spinning, drawing us,
down and into it;

but we resist.

I decided to risk it;
to let go;
to find out where the black hole deep within
me
would take me.

I let go of all my handholds,
and fell helplessly,
down, down, down,
deep into the black hole within me.
I spun around dizzily,
and the old handholds disappeared from sight.

Round and round,
down and down,
deep into the black hole within me...

And then
in the silence,
perfect peace, tranquility, calmness, serenity,
I was exploded out the other end!

And to my amazement and astonishment,
there I found all the others who also had let go
and decided to let God's black hole deep
within
bring them to Him.

On the other side is the *real* world, loving souls,
and God

Energy

How many lonely hurt people
must there be out there.

In allowing God to use me
to help others,
it seems that
with just the slightest bit of
concern, care, interest, love
from me,
people feel better,
seem encouraged, have hope,
are energized.

And, it seems,
people who need some
concern, care, interest, love,
are all about.

The way
it seems He helps them through me in some
small way
and the way doing so evokes
powerful emotions in me
including joy, love, satisfaction,
convinces me that

Loving another
energizes them
and opens me to
the energy of the Universe,
taps me into
God's energy.

And I don't need to look very far
for people
to help,
to love,
to energize;
they're all about me.

I trust the ripples will spread
to the far reaches
of the Universe.

Tears

It's almost as if the snow is crying.

Daytime is getting stronger,
staying longer;

The temperatures moderate,
and the air calms.

The Old Man
still controls,
All is covered in white;
and Torch is frozen solid,

But, is he weakening?
Is he tired?
Or is he simply resting,
in preparation
for the next storm?

There is no sign of any other life,
but why is the snow crying?

Are they tears of sorrow,
at the death of all those gone,
or tears of joy,
at the beauty of Winter's delight?

Surely, they are not
tears of hope
for life to come,
there is no sign of life hereafter
Winter.

But the tears flow,
drop by drop,
from roofs, from trees, from plants,
from all things covered
by his snow.

Why the crying?

Love

must be so plentiful
on this earth;
or else my family
is so well loved by others,
they don't need mine.

Why is it
family doesn't seem to treasure
the love given by family?
Too close?
Taken for granted?
Disbelieved?

If someone said to me,
Drive up North
and there I'll find
a loving person
who will love me
unconditionally,
just the way I am,
for the rest of my life,
no matter what I do,

I'D RUN UP NORTH IF I HAD TO!

Yet, here I am with such an offer,

and no one comes,
no one of my family,
that is.

They're either well loved enough,
don't really believe in my love,
or don't know
love's power or value.

Sounds like a familiar story,
doesn't it.

Thank God
there are those,
who need my love,
who want my love,
who value my love,
who love in return.
Thank God.

In Time

Torch,
frozen and crusted,
dotted by fishing shanties,
wind swept, snow covered, barren,
silent to the human ear,
but seething down below.

An old friend,
South Wind
sweeps up North
all the way from the Great Gulf
to say,
Hi old friend,
just as I tickle your waves
Northward in the Summer,
I will help you
conquer Winter's grip,
By sweeping his clouds away,
letting the Sun do its work,
and melting snow and ice.

Hi old friend
maybe not today,
although many of his troops
are fleeing in tears,
but hope is in the air.

Hi old friend,
let me warm your icy crust,
let me put all of winter's friends
on notice;
this may not yet be our time,
but our time is coming,
daylight is winning more time
each day,
I send temperatures soaring,
creation senses change,
though largely invisible,
or like snow's tears,
transparent.

Hi, my friend, Torch,
I hug and kiss you,
and understand your silent response,
caused by your temporary shell.

Hi, my friend,
Feel my warmth
and know that
the birds of spring
will join me soon,

that I bring hope.

South Wind

Never doubt the Power

of South Wind.

He sweeps in
from the Great Gulf
and in two days
ate up
nearly all of Winter's Work.

Ally of Torch,
he frightened off
all those
violating her
with fishing holes,
by
creating quickly-growing
ponds of water
on her crust.

Roofs were melted clean,
roads swept clear
and dry,
trees were blown clean,
and grass allowed
to see the sky again.

Gentle?
Most times, yes,

but this blow,
South Wind shows
his might,
gives Winter a bit of his own
right back at him.

Torch smiles
and knows again,
that South Wind
will free her
soon.

Warrior

Late in Coming,

Early in Departing,

but

Filled with Snow,
Chilled with Cold,

this Winter,
my Winter,

was

Powerful,
Intense,
Real,

A Warrior,

who came into the battle,
fought hard,
left his mark(s),

and departed

with
Honor.

Perspective

All this time,

I've been thinking people

could see things through my eyes,

hear things through my ears,

feel things with my heart.

Only now have I realized,

they cannot.

I used to think that

because of the correctness of my belief,

or the power of my argument or persuasion,

or because of their liking me

they could see things,

hear things,

feel things,

as I did

...or at least close.

I now know that's not possible;

their view, their sound, their feel,

is as colored by their eyes, ears, heart,

as is mine.

So how can I expect them to

see my view, hear my sound, feel my emotion,

any more

than I can see, hear, feel theirs.

Ha!

You thought I was finished,
spent.

South Wind came for a visit,
melted some snow,
let Sun warm you a bit,
tempted you with Spring and
you actually began to think
I was gone.

Ha!
Double Ha!

The Old Man
is not dead yet.

Feel North Wind again,
cold and icy.
See the snows again,
cover everything with white.
See those puddles on Torch
freeze over into ice.

Start the fires,
layer your clothing,
Old Man Winter is alive
and well.

I love late February
and even March;
added daylight doesn't scare me,
the cold gray just
makes my work more visible.

I feed on
your growing impatience with me.
I sense your tiredness
with my cold and snow.
I am determined
to use my allotted time
fully and with Gusto.

Dream on,
if you want,
of warmer times;
the Now is still mine.

I have seen Circles do their Work

Healing Circles,
Prayer Circles,
Sharing Circles,
Ritual Circles,
Ceremonial Circles,
Mystical Circles.

I have experienced their power

In Hospice,
in Grief Work,
at Gatherings of Men,
in Life in the Spirit Prayer Groups,
at Al-Anon meetings,
in simple sharings.

In safe
loving,
nurturing
circles of hearts,
people heal,
no,
God heals through people;
people are healed through each other,
by God.

In circles,
there is no head nor foot,
no top nor bottom
no chief nor chairman,
no barrier between,
no first or last
no beginning or end,
no structure or procedure,
no right or wrong,
only all
and
nothing,
together
in Love.

Circles
represent Nothing in the Now,
yet,
are complete.

Snow

so softens the night.

At least a foot of snow
has fallen,
but
not in anger or fury,
not with cold icy winds,
simply gently softly
kindly.

And
the snow is light.

As I push the shovel
across the patio,
it fluffs up
and around the shovel
which glides along
easily.

And
the snow softens
all the evening
sounds
and sights.

It's a gentle
winter night.

This must be
the gentle side
of the Old Man,
his sweet side,
the soft side.

He's almost lovable.

Trust

Once I turned it over to Him
in complete Faith and Trust,
He really took over.

Once I opened up to Creation,
I, not only began to appreciate its beauty,
but also, share in its energy.

Once I opened up to those around me,
I, not only loved them, and energized them,
but I was loved, energized.

Once I opened up,
I saw things I'd never seen before
in people I'd known a lifetime,
beautiful things,

including myself,

and God.

Once I followed the guidance He provided
every moment,
He took me on a mystical journey,

from person to person,

book to book,

poem to poem,

event to event,

and helped me to learn and grow and share

and love

all along the way.

Once I turned my life over to Him,
I felt Him living in me
while

I lived in Him.

This Morning

He blessed my Solstice,
my effort
to know myself and Him better.

He awoke me in time
to see
the beauty
of the

Full Moon Setting.

Through a misty haze,
the glowing moon
shone through to me
and warmed my soul,
told me
to follow the guidance
provided me
every moment.

It lasted only minutes

as it sank beneath the Western horizon

but left an indelible
mark on my soul,

for it was there for me;

it was another
visible beautiful sign

that my search was noble,

my journey valiant,

my course true.

Full Moon Setting,
Blessed by God.

Luna

The night belonged to the Moon

The winter winds
were silent,

The clouds
had moved on,

The stars
fought for attention,

But this night
belonged to

the Moon.

Nearly full,

it glowed graciously,

lighting up the countryside

and
giving the snow a glistening sparkle.

She
grew in size as
she began to set
on the Western horizon.

But jealous Sun

this night
would not allow her to
take a final bow alone;

Jealous mighty Sun
came on stage
before Moon could set

and

took away the contrast
against which

Moon did glow.
That night,
Moon bowed in daylight.

Well Done

He took my Winter Solstice,

my time of Contemplation,

my search for me, for Him,

My reaching out to others,

my poetry,
my journaling,
my eyes of God,
my photos of Creation,
my...
offering
and

Blessed them,
and said, "Well Done,"
with

the most beautiful

February Full Moon

ever seen.

What I've Learned

I have learned:

It is important for me to spend periods of time
away from the everyday scene,
and to forget that "there are things to do"
and that Nature offers me a special invitation,
asking nothing and encouraging me to be
who I am,
while symbolizing the beauty of all creation.

But, I have also learned:

that spending long periods of time alone
will never be my way to wholeness;
Life, for me, will always be found in
relationships,
wit people, with myself, with my interior.
Going away from others is valid for me, only if
in it I attain a quality of self-presence
that begins to meet the Divine,
which then flows out to others.

I have learned:

Reflective perception reveals for me
the hidden function of emotion.

Motion allows my body to speak;
the feelings of my body become available.

Massage helps me;
being cared for opens my needs to me.

Leisure is doing what I _feel_ like doing.

Journaling helps me,
especially if it helps experience the moment.

Interactions with others tells me
how and when and how often to
seek the inner companion,
who is lovable, self, and my gift to others.

I have learned:

Touching emotion and letting it permeate the
moment
is pivotal for me.
I am not frightened by emotion;
I do not fear being drowned in emotion;
I want to get into feelings.

Being with and for myself and others
takes precedence over
compulsively "doing"
in order to prove myself adequate.

I have learned:

When centered,
I do not experience an inner blankness,
a turning off of consciousness.

When centered,
I am awake and alert,
filled with an influx of emotions;
I am aware of myself in a new way
with a new experience of energy.
(These genuine emotions and spiritual energy
attract me to the interior.)

When centered,
I am awash with emotion,
I let myself be taken by the feelings
of each successive moment.

Life, inside and out, fills me with energy.
The interior world nourishes me,
Inner blankness fades,
Contemplation becomes real and desirable.

I have learned:

Coming together in prayer with others
is of special significance to me;
His Spirit accompanies the group
in this time;
The Holy Spirit is present in the group.
Although I gain no fervor in praying in group,
coming together in prayer is no mere ritual for
me,
it is an interior necessity,
Prayer in common is an urgent need,
as for me,
people are what life is all about.

I have learned:

In Thanksgiving

Dear God,

Thank You for the Winter Solstice,
for the time to listen.

Thank You for Torch,
for all the beautiful Trees,
for the snow,
for the winter creatures,
for the Days and Nights
and all the beauty in between.

Thank You for the bright Sun,
for the gracious Moon
lighting up the new fallen snow,
for all the stars shining in the sky,
for the winds,
North and South, West and East.

Thank You for the music
you have helped me find and
taught me to hear;
for the flutes,
for the drums,
and the praise they produce.

And Thank You for the silence
in which You speak to me.

Thank You for all the people
with whom You've had me connect.
Thank You for the messages You've given me
through them,
and for allowing me to touch them
on Your behalf.

Thank You for the Nows
in which You've allowed me to create
poetry,
journal,
Eyes-of-God;
and
Thank You for helping me
capture on film
a glimpse of Your Creation's beauty.

Dear God,
Thank You for painting for me
a million pictures
through my picture window
that I might foretell
what Heaven's all about.

Thank You for the readings
to which You've directed me;
they have inspired my soul.

Thank You for St. Luke's,
St. Joseph Prayer Group,
North Country Hospice,
The Gathering of Men,
and all the stepping stones
You've provided.

Thank You for my Guardian Angel,
Michael,
whose love I treasure,
and who's help I need
and will ever seek.
Thank You for our sense of humor.

Thank You for helping my children
along their journeys.
Thank You for helping Marilyn and me
along our ways.

Thank You for the Chateau,
a sacred place for me,
where You and I touched.

Thank You for the Great Tree,
and the friends we have become;
thank You for allowing me
to share its energy.

Dear God,
Thank You for Love;
for the power to love, and energize others,
and thus for allowing me
to be energized by the power of the universe,
by Your power.

Thank You
for multiplying whatever I gave You,
just like loaves and fishes;
You are, indeed,
The Great Multiplier and Provider.

Thank You for the Bibles
You have given me
to better know Your Word.

Thank You for
my new kitchen,
may Marilyn be pleased.
Thank You for the men
whose labor went into it,
may they be blessed by You
in thanksgiving.

Dear God,
Thank You for lessons learned,
to "go with the flow"
to "let go"
to love others "where they are"
that Your energy is in all things,
that Your guidance is all around me,
that my messages come through others,
that I am fulfilled in others,
in You, and not in solitude.

Thank You for Creation,
and
for making me a part of it,

Thank You for living in me
and
allowing me to live in You.

Dear God,

I thank You.

To Love
is to tap into
the Energy of the Universe,

God's Energy.

Views
Along the Way

Zen

Zen means meditation

Meditative attentiveness

A style of living
to overcome suffering

A receptive, less self-conscious, pliable
relation to the world

In Harmony
with the Seasons

Mind and Body not separate;
stillness of mind
achieved through
attention to body

Fostering Awareness

Letting Go of preoccupations

Like the parables of Jesus,
breaking thought patterns,
ingrained habits,
conventional wisdom
to reach

The Truth

A dysfunction?

A hierarchy
Whose identity comes from power and
patriarchy,
Not relationships and intimacy,
Imposing celibacy on its operatives
Without adequate support
Resulting either in

Sexual addiction

Or

Sexual anorexia

Barely bearable when viewed as
A charism of service to church,

Unbearable when imposed

By

A hierarchy

Not needing relationship and intimacy.

BATTLE

In this body
My Spirit struggles,
Not to escape
--this body is needed--
But to reach fulfillment,
To become whole,
To express itself,
To Love and be Loved,
To be united with its Creator.

My body, my mind,
Seem to ignore, even deny
My spirit's needs,
Wanting their needs fulfilled,
Their appetites satisfied.

The needs of my body and mind
Are not evil;
Devoting my whole life to them
Without allowing my spirit to grow
would be the great tragedy.

Time out, body;

Time out, mind!

Beatitudes as Gifts, not Tasks

I am poor spirit
When I do not feel entitled,
When I do not feel in control,
When I see all I have as gift.

My Blessing: Gratefulness

I mourn my losses
When I sit in silence and weep
When I help bereaved find their way.

My Blessing: Compassion

I am meek
When I challenge authority,
When I have no status to defend,
When I risk humiliation.

My Blessing: Freedom

I hunger and thirst for justice
When I am deeply aware of needs of others,
When I respond to the needs of others.

My Blessing: Profound Awareness

I am merciful
When I treat my injurer better than they
deserve,
When I act with kindness towards my offender.

My Blessing: Kindness

I am pure of heart
When I see things as they are, not as I am,
When I see straight to the Heart of God.

My Blessing: Vision

I am a peacemaker
When I know I am not right,
When I seek the truth of another,
When I know truth exists beyond what I know,
When I am willing to keep learning.

My Blessing: Openness

I suffer persecution
When I am ridiculed for my ways,
When I am labeled a soft touch
for being poor in spirit,
When I am called too sensitive
for being a mourner,
When I am called a fool for being meek,
When I am called naïve for being merciful,
When I am called a heretic for being a
peacemaker.
I am the Blessing.

Body and Soul

My body
is my Relationship to the World,
to Others.
It is my Life
as Communion.
Everything of my body is created for
Relationship.
Love,
the highest form of Communion,
finds its incarnation
in my body.
My body
sees, hears, feels,
and thus,
leads me out of isolation in myself.
My body
is not my dark side,
not prison of my spirit,
but rather
its Freedom.

My Body is
My Soul as Love,
My Soul as Communion,
My Soul as Life,
My Soul as Movement.

Boundaries

are useful,

and often necessary in life.

But some are created
as part of our addiction for security,
our addiction for approval,
our addiction for power.

And some boundaries
become barriers;
barriers to Growth,
barriers to Relationship—true Relationship.

Thank God

for my dreams and desires

as they know no bounds.

If God judges me
not so much on what I've accomplished,
but more on what I desire,

then I will reach the horizons

I seek

even if crossing boundaries.

A Call

Move beyond being Roman.
Remain Catholic, but no longer Roman.
Tradition has no real energy.
Institutional church is engaged in self idolatry
with little hope for true renewal and reform.
Do not hold off personal growth awaiting
institutional reform.

Embrace our historical sacramental tradition
of discovering the sacred in the ordinary
with powerful objects, words and movement,
powerful prayer and rituals.
Believe in a God present to us,
not distant "in the sky."
Embrace Jesus as one path to the sacred.
Believe that we each must find our path in
community to nurture and sustain us.

Jesus preached a Reign of God most manifest
in service to one another,
filled with healing for each and the world,
empowered by unconditional love.
This love leads us all to justice and peace.
Revelation is ongoing
and we are part of creating
the new revelation for all,
that the Reign of God calls us all to freedom
and justice and peace.

"Religion and Spirituality" are primarily about
how we live in community
so all can live in dignity with justice and peace.
Religion is not about salvation and saving our
souls,
but freedom from all oppression,
freedom to embrace God's great love and
share it with all humanity.

Institutions, primarily religious institutions, exist to
help us discover the sacred in the ordinary,
and live the life-giving holiness in family, work
and community.

Leave a suffocating institution to find freedom
and sacredness of life.

*Paraphrased from the Sharing
of a Dear Friend, Tim*

Change

The notion that

Humanity is in a state of "becoming,"
That
We are "in process,"

Poses a threat
To those who are in power,
Those who wish to cling to power.

Christianity is a "Movement,"
A "Transformation."

So, the Eucharist

Must be constantly reinvigorated

To be relevant to people in their own cultures;

Unjust social attitudes and structures

Must be challenged if they diminish people;

Patterns of domination and oppression,

Outside and within the Church,

Must be opposed.

Church

If we choose to believe
that in choosing the twelve
from among all the disciples,
Jesus intended to create
a *structured* community,

we do not have to believe
that the community exists
only when the structure exists.

The coming into being
of Church
was/is a *dynamic* process,
likely gestating in Jesus' mind,
not fully developed at His death,
not fixed for eternity,

and ever changing

in response to the movement of

The Holy Spirit.

Church Awry

Why does the principle of subsidiarity,
An essential element of Catholic Social
Teaching,
Take a back seat to

The Institution's need to perpetuate itself?

Why is Class Struggle by the poor,
With whom the Catholic Church espouses
solidarity,
Often ignored or condemned
So the Institution can protect internal cohesion.

Why is human dignity,
A cornerstone of Catholic Teaching,
Abused and contradicted with action

By the need to protect
Institutional Authority?

Why is solidarity with the poor,
The stated preference of the Catholic Church,
Overwhelmed by bishops' penchant for the
affluent and powerful

In order to protect
the Institution's economic base?

Why are Freedom of Religion
And Primacy of Conscience,
Boldly proclaimed as Catholic fundamentals,
Offered only to non-Catholics

In order to maintain Institutional Order?

Why is Non-Discrimination and Inclusiveness,
As exampled by Jesus Christ,
Only Selectively applied by an all-male
celibate hierarchy

To maintain
an all-male celibate controlled
Institution?

Why is the Good News
we are commissioned to spread

made subservient

to maintenance of the Institution
established to spread it?

Church From Below

Kung Inspires:

Believable without being Authoritative
Intellectual without being Arrogant
Bubbling and Boiling

Let us resist by
Celebrating Last Supper Services Together
Not Willing to Wait.

If the Faithful could Vote
Issues would have been resolved
years ago.

Vatican's consciousness of Power
is the problem.

Playing games with the Eucharist
in order to
keep authoritative standing of church in tact
has nothing to do with Jesus

Jesus would banish the authoritarians
same as money changers.

Future:

No will be scared to have to accept an
infallible pope;

No one will do without Eucharist.

How can Vatican advocate peace with Islam
when not finding
Peace within Christianity?

Where are Women in the Church?

Isn't God female?

Issues will be resolved.

Climbing

Climbing the Mountain of Life,

We can use doctrines, dogmas, and creeds,

to help pull us up over difficult obstacles,

as long as we then untie ourselves from them

to keep growing.

We don't need permanent hitching posts,

which keep us from reaching our peak.

Tradition offers us

a good footing

from which to move on.

If we simply look around

for others to help up,

Love and Compassion

will push us and pull us

Upward.

Cloud of Unknowing

I experience God in two ways,

in the positive experiences of life
and
in the negative.

God exists in both,
not only because of God's Transcendence,
but also because of God's Immanence.
In the positive aspect,

I witness God in all of Creation;

In the negative,
I witness what God is Not.

I move to Mystical Union
by rejecting all my thoughts
about who I am and Who God is.

I move to Mystical Union
by moving away from thoughts and feelings
about me
so I can begin to focus on the Divine alone.

I discover that
My True Self
exists only in God.

Connect

When True Soul mates connect,
When Lovers truly Love each other,

Both Grow.

Neither is Master
or better,

Both are Masters for each other,
Students of
One an other.

Their Love
for each other
Only flows freely 'tween them,
as they Each
see themselves
as Beautiful Creations of God

and Loveable.

Both are Lovers
and
Each is Beloved.

Continuity

Am OK with change;
It goes hand in hand with Growth;
Lack of it is a sign of death.

Yet, humans seem to also need continuity,
Connectivity with things past.

But what if what some believe is true,
Namely that each moment is created anew,
That each moment
bears no relationship to prior,
That there is no such thing as
Cause and Effect?

Scary, indeed.
But oh so freeing.

I could live in each new moment
Without the pasts' burdens,

Enjoying God's creations anew afresh
Being Reborn in the Divine each moment.

I would
Be truly free from all things past
To Love fully
Without ties that existed
In prior moments now long disappeared.

I wonder . . .

Creation

Creation is an expression of God's Love.

It's distinction is its Gratuity.
It is a Free Gift of Love with no strings attached.
Else it would be imperfect.

God gives the world to itself,
as the place where humans live out our destiny
to be
human.

Made in the image and likeness of God,
we have the potential
to Love as God Loves
in the real world.

We have to make the world
a more truly human reality,
failing through fear or greed,
succeeding through courage and generosity.

The Sacred
is not something God imposes
on top of secular history,
or
Grace producing a supernatural dimension
of the human person
grafted upon a secular original.

There is one history;
The Church is a worldly reality.
Our Desire for God
is not grafted on to our secular base,
but is a Natural Expression
of Humans as created by God.

The secular
is not some godless reality
requiring some special Divine Act
to open it to the Holy.

The secular is already Graced.
Nature is Graced.
The world is already Sacred
(whether or not we know it.)
Grace is everywhere.

The world and human beings
are already open to the infinite,
especially when they follow the natural order.

The humanization of the world,
by whomever,
is the world growing into
God's Plan.

Our struggle toward
A Fuller Humanity
is
Salvation History.

We are secular beings.
We live and breathe in the world.
The world lives and breathes in us.
We are people in a human world.
We are organisms in a material universe.
We live simultaneously
in a world of meanings
and
causes and effects.

The struggle for meaning
and
The Experience of Chaos
are inescapably
part of the secular reality.

Any religion that suggests
the world is not our home
misreads Incarnational Theology.

We are born, live, and die
within the secular world.
Being religious
cannot be something that relativizes
the secularity
that is part of our very being.

Crisis

The crisis
of institutional Church

is the autistic notion that

The Sacramental World
is contained and controlled solely within
the members of the hierarchy;

that they are the chosen ones,
called from eternity

to save Church by supervising it.

The institutional hierarchy
are so focused on their own centrality,
that they distort
Sacraments.

Instead of richly human Sacramentality,
sensual, sexual and spiritual,

They abuse the Body of Christ
by closing and merging our churches and
by deforming personality into
antagonistic elements of spirit and flesh,

attempting to foist on us
"antidotes" for being human,

rather than
Sacraments which nourish and nurture
our full humanity.

We are being offered

not the ecstasy and passion of
Teresa of Avila or
John of the Cross,

not the Excitement of Transformation,

but instead

ceremonies

paved with the literal
rather than the sacramental,
laced with chords of law and precedent
rather than the lyrical,
void of mystery borne by story or symbol.

But,

a renewal of the Sacramental Life
of institutional Church

requires

a Truthful, Open, Collegial Relationship
with
God's People.

Dear Dad,

Did I ever give you the impression

that I thought I was better than you

because of all my formal education
(of which you had virtually none)

or because of all my financial success
(of which you could not even dream)

while you were alive?

Dad,

In my immaturity,

I may have actually felt that way,

and even, on occasion,

acted that way.

Can you ever please forgive me?

You were a truly Loving and Wise man,

and although I am striving

to stand proudly on your shoulders
and carry my Spiritual Growth

beyond that of all of our ancestors,

I admire and respect

everything about you

and am thankful

that in all of our years together,

I can recall

not one single discouraging word.

You always went along with me

and supported me

in whatever I tried to accomplish.

I now know

this is one of the Greatest Gifts

a parent can give a child,

Unending Love, Support, and Encouragement.

Thanks, Dad.

The Deep

The Greatest Treasures
seem to buried in the depths.

Gospel Truths
are hidden in the parables;
Pearls,
in Oyster beds;
Diamonds,
deep below the earth's surface;
Rare Orchids,
hidden in the forests;
New Human Life,
Entrusted in the depths
of a Woman's Womb;

Our True Self,
deep below our consciousness;

The Culture of a People,
buried in Myths and Feats.

Nothing worth finding
seems revealed easily.

Mystery is not Unknowable;
Mystery is Infinitely Knowable.

Dis-integration

My sensuality is not unspiritual!

My growth

depends on re-integrating

my substance and my spirituality.

My sins have resulted from

the fracturing of my sensuality

from my substance united to God.

I have been dis-integrated

from my substance

and have caused injury

to myself and others.

My search for the Divine

is a journey within

a re-turning, a turning back

to the unity in which I was created.

Ear of the Heart

St. Benedict agreed to lead a community.

He asked for strict Silence at night.

Benedict saw prayer as a form of
Listening.

He asked people to Listen with
The Ear of the Heart.

To Listen
was Benedict's only hard and fast instruction.

He asked that
spoken prayers be short.

He did not want us to be
such chatterboxes
that God couldn't get a word in edgeways.

"God regards our hearts and tears
and not our many words."

"Harden not your Hearts."

For Benedict,
ear and heart are joined together.

With silence,
and Loving Listening,
Benedict believed,
Our Hearts will swell
with unspeakable sweetness of
Love.

Benedict espoused
Humility, Stability, and Hospitality.

Quiet Self-Confidence.

Eleventh Insight

My prayer energy is real;
it flows out from me
and
affects the world.

I take in energy from the Creator
and send it out
to others.

Through increased perception,
I breathe in a higher level of energy
with my increased awareness of
the beauty around me
a measure.

The higher level of energy,
the more beauty I see.

I visualize the high level of energy
flowing out of me
with Love as the measure.

I use the outgoing energy flow
to increase the synchronistic flow of my life,
by staying constantly alert
and expecting the next coincidence
that moves my life along.

My expectation
sends the energy out even farther,
making it even stronger.

I expect that my prayer-field
boosts the energy in others
lifting them to a connection to
the Divine within
and
into higher self-intuition.

I maintain my energy outflow
despite fear or anger.

I always seek a positive outcome.

I strive
to keep negative thoughts out of my head
regarding other people.

I acknowledge angels
and
empower them
to help me
and others
in all situations.

In this,
humanity will reach
its spiritual destiny.

Emmaus and Me

*Something prevented them
from recognizing Him.*

My own agenda,
My own attachments,
My own need for control
blinds me.

*Our own hope had been
that he would set Israel free.*

I conformed Him to my image,
expected Him to do my bidding,
to respond to my pleas.

*You must be the only one in Jerusalem
who does not know what's happening there.*

I see world events
through my eyes,
not in the eyes of the suffering,
not in terms of God's will.

*Was it not ordained
that Christ should suffer
and enter into His Glory?*

I spent so much of my life
avoiding sorrow,

avoiding suffering,
looking for the Good Life.
He took the bread and said the Blessing,
He broke it handed it to them.
Their eyes were opened
and they recognized Him . . .

Do I truly see Jesus in the Eucharist?
Am I transformed in the reception?
Do I open my table to all?
Do I see every meal
as liturgy?

Did not our hearts
burn within us
as He talked to us on the road
explaining Scripture?

I treasure the moments
when my heart so burns,
but do not often enough
open my heart and mind
to listen.

I must listen, and be
Open and Aware.

Words to End a Relationship

Forgive me.

I forgive you.

Thank You.

I Love You.

Good Bye.

Evangelize or Not?

It seems to me:

The Religions of the world
affirm an Ultimate Reality,
which they conceive and name
in different ways
and which
transcends the material universe
and
is immanent within it.

While this Ultimate Reality
is beyond the scope
of complete human understanding,
many seemed to have experienced
Its Presence
in diverse ways
some of which have given rise
to the world's religions.

The world's great Religions,
including their different
and sometimes incompatible teachings,
offer authentic paths to
The Supreme Good.

The world's religions
share many basic values,
such as

Love, Compassion, Justice, and Honesty.
Some religions
are misused
for purposes contrary to the
core values.

Each person
must follow his/her own conscience;
the possibility of conversion
is part of a human right
to religious freedom.

Traditional assertions
of exclusive possession of
absolute truth
repel people
who seek the Wisdom
that other religions offer.

Major efforts
on the part of one religion
to convert those of another religion
to their beliefs
may be misdirected.

Dialogue among peoples
of different religions
who wish to learn and benefit
from another's inheritance and insights,
and not evangelization,
should be the driving force
for relationships among peoples.

There is a need
to heal historic antagonisms
between people of different religions.

Let it begin with me.

Father-Son-Father

Why such high expectations of a Father
by his Son?

Why such resentment of a Father's
weaknesses and failings
by his Son?

Does a Son dislike his own failings
he also or only sees in his Father?

Does a Son wish
his Father had helped him
be more than he is?

Does a Son see too much of himself
in his Father?
or too much of his Father
in himself?

Why when a Father is so proud of his Son,
cannot a Son be proud of his Father

until he is gone?

Why are so many beautiful and necessary
sharings
withheld
until Father—or Son—is gone?

A Son can succeed
with or without his Father's help;
Are a Son's failures
attributable to his Father?

We can accept
others will not be as we'd like,
yet why can't we seem to give
a Father
that same acceptance?

I Love my Father;
I Love my Sons,

Unconditionally.

Fear

On one hand

I fear the unknown,
The possible dire consequences
of my actions,
The possible harm that might come to me.

On the other hand,

My Faith is to sustain me;
I am to fear naught of this world
In the knowledge of my eternal sprit.

My life is to be driven by Love,

Not Fear.

Then again, on the other hand,

Avoiding fear can mean

Avoiding new ventures,
Not trying new things,
Staying complacent.
Fear seems a natural part of life's journey.

To fear or not to fear,
Is that the Question?

Fine

I asked how she was,
really wanting to know.

She gave me the word that
she gave so many others
seeming to answer their query
without revealing anything.

She told me
she was

Fine.

I was puzzled.

Did she mean she was
"free from impurity"?

I believed her but was not really trying to go
there.

Did she mean she was
"thin"?
(Honestly she sure did not look it.)

Did she mean she was
"not coarse or rough"?

I never thought she was.

Did she mean she was
"very small"?

Perhaps she was feeling so.

I did not think she meant that
she was
"very precise or accurate"
for if she were,

"fine" did not help me much.

Perhaps she meant that
she was
"delicate, subtle, or sensitive"

which I could understand
given her loss.

Was she telling me
she felt
"superior"?

Hmmmmm

I doubted she meant to say
she was

"ornate"

as it did not show.

Maybe she meant
she was
"keen"

which is great given her situation.

Was she telling me
she was
"refined"?

(Always thought she was.)

I wonder if she meant that
she was feeling
"powdery or pulverized"?

How could I help?

I'm really hoping
she meant that
she was feeling

"dandy, first-class, first rate, five-star,
top-notch"

but somehow
I think if she were,

she'd have used those words.

She told me,

"I'm fine,"

and

I have no idea how she is.

I'd better tell her

I *really* want to know.

Fork

Either Path of the Fork
Brings
Danger, Risk, Pain
And
Joy, Fulfillment, and Growth.

Taking neither path,
Choosing to reside in
Indecision at the Fork,
Avoids pain,
Risks nothing,
EXCEPT Growth.

Ultimately,
All paths lead to the same Destination,
With Forks all along the way
Defeating Travelers who
Do nothing,
Risk nothing,
Choose neither,
Grow not.

Though each Path
Provides experiences needed
And
Treasures with Dangers,
I cannot travel both.

And so it is

I cannot take both

I dare not take neither

The path I must take

Is clearly

Either.

Goal

If someone gifted you with

An all-expense paid trip

To a beautiful, exciting destination

for three weeks,

But required

that you bring nothing back with you,

Would you
Spend much time
Acquiring things?

Or would you devote your time

And effort

To enjoying all

The experience had to offer?

*

Well?

Grace

I never started out, nor ever dreamt, to be
a spiritual guide or emotional companion
for those on life's Grief Journey.

It has been pure Grace.

It came about because I was given
the immense privilege and gift
of being taken
inside the lives of the countless people
I have met
in my Grief and Spiritual Growth Ministries.

What brought us into kinship
was the discovered God-given ability
to travel inward,
to connect the inner experience with
the outer experience,
and to trust that the Divine
is found in all of Life's experiences.

The willingness to be *open to Growth*,
to keep *climbing the Mountain of Life*,
to give self over to
Transformation
by continual *Attentiveness* to
the movement of the *Holy Spirit* in our lives
has changed many of my fellow travelers
and in the process me.

Great Lesson

I have a Soul.

Having a Soul means To Pray.

To Pray is to Actualize a Virtue
and at the same
Sow its Seeds.

First: Resignation to the Will of God
(Acceptance of my Destiny
insofar as
I cannot and should not change it)

This must become second nature to me.
(There is always something
I cannot escape.)

Correlating to this attitude is
Trust.
I find God disposed to come to my aid,
but not always as I expect.

But I must offer to others
what I expect from God.

In giving me the gift of
resignation to God's Will,
I am also given the right
to ask for God's help

but only if

I have gratitude.

I can ask nothing of God
if I lack gratitude.

To be truly thankful, however,

I must be conscious of
All the Good God has given me.

I must appreciate even the smallest gifts.

Gratitude is the complement of Supplication
just as
Generosity is the complement of Trust in God.

My relationship with the world
depends essentially on

My relationship with God.

The Greatest Battle

The Greatest Battle I fought
and fight daily
is resisting the temptation

to try and be the person

everyone around me wants me to be

rather than the person

I am meant to be,

the person I was created to be.

My ultimate accountability relates to

fully becoming my true self

in the face of all the expectations by others
to be what they want.

Attempting to fulfill
those expectations is futile anyway,

while the journey of true self-discovery,
albeit painful and difficult,
is the essence of life.

Guidance

To move my children
beyond the law of the Old Testament;
To dispel their notion
of an angry vengeful Divine Father;
To Free them
from the tedious judgment of others;
I became At-One
with them,
preaching
and
Living

Love, Compassion, Mercy, Forgiveness,
Inclusiveness.

So that there would be
No Confusion
about My Essential message,
I walked My talk.

So what do they do?

They
set up
hierarchies,
rules, regulations, systems,
bureaucracies,

which

reinforce fear,
exclude people,
deny freedom,
judge others,
discriminate,
demonstrate a lack of love.

They have become the only kind of people
I reviled,

the pharisitical,

those judging all others,
believing they had exclusive access to the
truth,
Church Hierarchists.

Hard Drive Installation

I've decided to install *Love*
on my system

I must first open my *Heart folder*

But several other programs are running:
Past/Hurts
Low Self-Esteem
Grudges/Resentment
Personal Agenda

No problem,
Love
Erases past hurts from Operating System,
Remains in permanent memory,
Overrides Low Self-Esteem with High version

But Grudges/Resentment and
Personal Agenda
must be turned off
as they prevent *Love* being installed

I go to the Start Menu and
Run *Forgiveness;*
Grudges and Resentment are erased

I go to Programs Menu and
Uninstall My Personal Agenda;
Making space for Others

Love begins installing,
but only base program

Upgrades are available by
Connecting with other Hearts
Error Message:
Missing files
I need to find
Self Acceptance
Self Forgiveness
Self Worth
loading them into my Heart folder
I need to delete
Self-criticism
Unworthiness
New files are loading
Smile
Laughter
Peace
Joy
Contentment

Love is Freeware
and
must be downloaded to all

Hope?

Is my hope delusion?

I guess True Hope
lies beyond my knowledge,
beyond my passion.

My hope often conflicts

with darkness,
with desperation,
with my own ignorance.

I guess Hope
is not a perpetual euphoria
where tragedy, nor anguish exist.

I know
I cannot attain a sense of optimism
by suppressing reality.

I'm sure True Hope
transcends all tragedy. I
Hope!

Humus

Earthy

Humility

Humor

Humanity

Earthy

In my Humility,
I know that I am simply an instrument,
not the source of any Healing

Laughing at myself
I can help others Laugh
and bring Healing
through Humor

In my Humanity,
I am less than perfect
but full of Love

Earthy

Humility-Humor-Humanity

Irony

As I am willing
and able

to Love others freely
without the need to know the impact

and

without expectation of Love in return,

I am truly Loved,

(though not necessarily by
ones I love.)

When I sought Love,
When I was needy of it,
When I required it,

I was incapable of
being loved,

perhaps because,

my focus was on me
and not

an other

Joined

Once I become a member of an organization
or institution,

its goals, objectives, aims, boundaries
become mine.

I identify with it
and
it tends to identify me.

Unfortunately,
Over time,
However lofty
the initial goals and objectives,

they always seem to
gravitate towards

perpetuating the institution
as it is
and protecting the position(s)
of those in control.

I thus find myself
defending the institution as it is
and helping those in power
stay in power.

No! I refuse.

On My Journey Path

hiking,   running,
skipping,
jumping,
climbing,
tr trip p ping,

f
a
l
l
i
n
g,

c r a w l i n g,

walking,   LeApInG,
spinning~gninnips

dancing, dancing

step . . . step . . . stepping . . .

BEING
DOING
LOVING
LIVING

On my Journey Path

just standing still

looking, watching, seeing
listening, hearing
breathing, smelling, tasting
touching, feeling,

holding,

letting go . . .
EXPLORING
PERCEIVING
AWARE
BEING
DOING
LOVING
LIVING
On My Journey Path

time to sit and rest

numb, still, rest,
quiet, peace,
silence
alone
lonely, sad,
hurting, painful,
crying, weeping
empty, grieving, dying

SPIspiritRIT

tugging, digging,
pulling, planting,
Gardening
Soning
Reigning
Watering, waiting, watching, waiting . . .

reflecting, meditating, praying,
reading, thinking, realizing,
listening, lingering, learning,

growing - GROWING
hungry, thirsty,
longing, yearning
wanting, learning,

knowing
growing - GROWING

aching, desiring, determining
feeding, nourishing, nuturing

growing

watering, watching, waiting . . .

sensing, feeling, thinking, learning,
understanding . . . .or not!

believing, trusting,
leaning, grasping, holding . . .
STANDING . . .
LETTING GO . . .
standing
knowing
growing
GROWING
KNOWING

On My Journey Path

stepping,
walking,
hiking,
BELIEVING
TRUSTING
GROWING
KNOWING
LEARNING
EXPLORING
PERCEIVING
AWARE
BEING
DOING
LOVING
LIVING

NOW !

Offered by Martha Williams

A Journey Through Grief

I have grieved
each of the losses in my life
differently.

I seem to grieve my losses
differently than do others.

As my losses are unique and
I am unique
so
I guess, my grief is unique.

Working through Grief
is the most difficult thing I have ever done.

Only in facing my pain,
and going with it,
have I been able to grow in it.
If I did not face it,
the pain simply
waited for me.

Denying the sorrow and pain
does not work;
Trying to avoid them
with overwork or other addictions
simply deferred the inevitable.

My Grief Journeys have been long and
difficult.

With my losses,
I have grown in trust of God
and now rely on God's help
in ways I'd never dreamt.

I may seem the same on the outside,
but inside,
I am different.
But I cannot explain how I am different;
for words fail.

Grace
now enables me to live with
paradox, conflict, unanswered questions, and
ambiguity.

My losses
brought me significant disturbance
at my surface
forcing me to seek and find
God's Love and Peace in my depths.

Peace seemed to come
with my ability and willingness
simply to say "yes" to God.

My "yes" to God
pulled me beyond myself
and my immediate loss.

I began to find and live with
the certainty that
my trust in God is greater than
my problems.

God's Love
illuminated my resistance, weakness, fear.
I learned to let them go,
albeit slowly and painfully.

I had to learn that
my journey through Grief
did not depend on me alone,
that God was helping me
through the Love and Concern
of others.

The people who helped me
were friends and
unexpected strangers.

Often they helped because
of their own experience
of hurts and wounds.

They knew that sharing sorrow
makes it less burdensome
and less painful.

People who brought me Love
were signs of
God's hidden presence.

Helping others is an Art,
a noble and sensitive art,
bringing healing and growth,
not only for me, but
also to my caregivers.

Others' walking with me
was most important for me,
more so than talking,
as words often were inadequate.

Others helped me,
not with their Wisdom,
but through the mysterious workings of Grace.

Wounded healers
ended up teaching me
about God.

I found God's gifts
more by walking with others
and sharing God's wonder,
than though talking.

I leaned that
God was/is present
in every situation in my life,
but that often
I had to look carefully to find God.

When others shared their vulnerability with me,
we discovered God in our midst.

When others let go
of trying to fix or change me or my situation,
we discovered deep beautiful places
in our hearts.

Empathy required much Listening.
Others' empathy
opened our hearts
where we discovered sanctuaries
of peace.

There, I found God.

It was hard to be open and receptive
when I felt wounded and hurt.
When pain was raw
in its newness,
finding hope was difficult.
My pain was so overwhelming
I only saw the fact of my loss.

God
seemed distant.
The good news of faith
was nowhere to be found
in the bad news of my loss.

The light from Grace
did not appear suddenly.
It grew in intensity
as I was able to persevere in
blind trust.

The light increased
as the sun at dawn,
with only significant objects visible
and details shadowed
and blurred.
I suffered misinterpretations
for want of light.

With more sunlight,
details became more distinct
with their importance realized.
By the High Noon of my journey,
all was revealed.

With a clearer view
of my own wretchedness,
I could begin to empathize
with the wretchedness of others,
hidden till now.

Preoccupation with my Grief
took me in two directions:
I faced bitterness, pessimism, and fear
because of my loss.
I felt cheated, overwhelmed, and trapped.
I imagined and expected the worst.

The dread
influenced how I acted.
These thoughts further isolated me
without me even knowing it.
How could I see God in such thoughts?

I began to find God as I picked up the pieces
of my life.
I began to see alternatives and opportunities
despite my heartache.
I learned to avoid focusing on
what happened to me
and instead
to concentrate on
what to do with what happened to me.

God brought light out of darkness,
order out of chaos,
meaning out of meaninglessness,
life out of death.

I had to stop ruminating on
things I could not change.
God gave us responsibility for
what God had created.
Yes, I was bewildered
by the tragic events of my losses,
but God was there.

God seemed distant and silent to me,
But God was/is there/here.

As I journeyed through my Grief,
I learned to live more
in the Present Moment.
I found joy
in who I was right now.
I no longer think about the future
as a source of happiness or peace.
It is Now.

Peace and Happiness
are not back there where I was;
nor in front waiting for me;
Peace and Happiness
lie within my heart
and increase or decrease
based on how I live my life
Now.

I keep on learning
to be fully alive
to the present moment.

And as I learned more
who I am
at the center of my heart
and saw and appreciated
my uniqueness,
I saw and appreciated the uniqueness of
others,
no longer expecting them
to be like me.

My Losses in life
are real,
but so is God.

I prayed,
I listened,
I lived one day at a time,
one moment at a time.

God entered my loss,
transforming it,
transforming me.

I found out that
Hope is not just an optimistic attitude;
It is an outlook
of mind and of heart.

I learned that
in the midst of deep sadness and suffering
Steadfast Love Transforms.

So much has been given me,
I have no more time
to dwell on
what
I have lost.

Key

The Key
to
Spirituality

is
Uncovering the very real
Interconnectedness
that makes Creation One

and
Finding our own place
in the Flow of Life,

Entering

The Mystery

and

Becoming part of
The Universal Dance.

The dynamic flow between creatures
is
The Fundamental Reality
and

We all have role in its pattern and stream.

Lay Minister Hurting

Tickets, tickets, tickets!

Can I have a ticket to the Church banquet?

No.
They have all been given to
the "worthy" servants of God.

You know;
the Ordained Ones,
the ones who have received
the "laying on of hands."

But, he put His hands on me too.

But, I am not ordained;
ordained by whom?

He is proud of me;
He Loves me;
He knows my value

But, no tickets—
for the un-ordained.

Excluded!
Marginalized!

These things don't usually happen in my life;
only in my Church.

Don't they realize
my ticket was given at Baptism?

And I was Validated
at my Commissioning.

I know that;
He knows that.

No tickets;
for the un-ordained.

Did I hear the Gospel message wrong?

Jesus includes all;
me too!
Jesus Loves me.
No tickets!

Jesus invited me to the banquet;
I know it.
But am I told, "Just Be submissive;

You're only a lay minister
(and a woman too.)

*(She was not allowed to join the funeral meal
of a loving friend—a Bishop.)*

Life is for Giving

In hell, one is reassured by the devil,
to relax and enjoy yourself.
Fire and brimstone, the devil says,
are superstition.
No one works in hell;
With no physical body
and no passage of time,
residents can act without consequence.
In hell, there is no hope, hence,
no duty, no work,
nothing to be gained by praying,
nothing to be lost by doing what you like.
Hell is the place
where there is nothing to do
but amuse yourself.

And if one tires of fantasy,
one can elect to live in heaven,
home of those who long to
master reality rather than ignore it.

Work belongs in Heaven
and the true joy in life
consists in completely giving yourself
to an overriding goal,
to a mighty cause.

Being human
is not the pursuit of money,
power, prestige, or possessions,
but
turning one's back on
personal aggrandizement
for the benefit of others.

To feather one's nest,
no matter the cost to others,
is the wrong purpose.

It is not so much the wrong purpose
as No Purpose in life.

Making money is not a goal;
Accumulating possessions is not a goal;
Personal profit and pleasure are not goals.

We all need an overriding Goal
to guide us,
something worth living for.

Nothing will satisfy us
except the happiness of others.
Treat others as Family,
and spend your time and energy
giving, giving,
and giving more.

We don't realize how joyous
this is.

Giving to make others happy
is
emotionally, physically, spiritually
satisfying.

Work
is a biological necessity;
Human Beings have an innate need
to give.

When I forget myself
in the happiness of those around me
I glow with Life and Beauty.

When I brood on myself,
I deteriorate,
physically, mentally, intellectually, and
spiritually.

The personal motive
debases humans.

Our best work
is motivated by Love.

Learning to Live for Others
is the very purpose of our existence.

We have been entrusted
to use the assets given us
for the greatest benefit of all.

We are sent
to enrich the life of others.

We must work down the debt
incurred taking life
for ourselves.

We must begin balancing the books.

Spiritual Awareness
can only come
when we have begun to wipe out
the debts of our self-focus.

But our giving must be selfless,
without ego.

Without Personal Relationships
this cannot be done.
We have to be in the midst of Others.

The purpose of selfless service
is not only to benefit others,
but also
to remove the obstacles to Love
in our own consciousness.
There is no way to do that,
except in Relationship.

When we give selflessly,
we beat a trail into
the depths of our consciousness.

Running after profit and pleasure,
we stunt ourselves.

Merging ourselves in a cause
greater than us,
for others,
opens us up
to real Growth.

Stop being
a selfish little clod
of ailments and grievances
complaining that the world
will not devote itself
to making me happy.

Suffering and Unhappiness
help me to grow.
Grief is the Gateway
to the Sacred.

All of us
come from God,
exist in God,
return to God.

Lost

Often we keep looking

for something we lost

in the place where we lost it

even though it's not there.

We look where we are

because that's where we are

even though what we seek is not.

Usually,

We must forget it

or look elsewhere.

Love's Lesson

Making my way through life,
Accomplishing whatever I accomplished
to work my way up the Mountain that is Life

demanded some courage, strength, smarts,
and commitment.

Despite knowing that
God's hand was guiding me all along,
I felt I needed to be strongly pro-active
to accomplish all I have.

But now,
In the bosom of
An all-powerful unconditional Love,

I am totally helpless.
In the midst of this raging inferno that is Real
Love,
I feel like a new born babe,
totally dependent on
She who Loves me.

The Love surrounds me,
Permeates me,
Defines me.

I am Captured by Love
And
Never wish to Leave.

Mind

Problem is not so much
that my mind can lead me astray.

Bigger Problem is
that I let my mind lead me anywhere.

I know I am not body;
I am learning I am not my mind.

I am so much more:

Eternal Spirit.

Yet so much of my life's effort
has been strictly "mental"

ignoring all

the beautiful rest of me.

Thank God
I have been able to move

my religious practice

out beyond my mind.

Move On

John begot

Nicholas
and Peter
and Mae
and Betty

begot

John Nicholas
and James

begot

Matthew Nicholas
and Mark
and Jacqueline
and Jerome

begot

Nicholas Alexander.

It's now seems OK

to move on . . .

My Spirituality/Sexuality

My Spiritual needs are my Human needs
are my Spiritual needs

I was created Sensual
I was made for
Anticipation, Stimulation, Revelation

I wonder through
Sight, Sound, Taste, Touch, Smell

I Thirst, Hunger, Yearn, Desire

Sacraments, for me,
are filled with Exhilaration,
arousing my
Creative Energies
that bring and Enlarge Life

Sacraments, for me,
Transcendentally Enflame
my human sensations

I am never moved thoroughly
without being moved
Sexually

I have never created anything
without engaging
My Sexuality

Sacraments, for me,
are Experiences of Intimacy

Sacraments, for me, are
Dynamic, Invasive,
Disruptive of One Stage of me,
Bearing a Newer and Richer Re-Integration,
Re-Membering me to
Wholeness
also known as
Holiness

When I can die
to some old part of myself,
surrendering all,
I have a chance to
Rise Anew,
More Integrated,
More Whole,
More Complete

For me,
It is impossible to separate
Sacramental from Sexual,
Sexual from Spiritual

Reconciliation, for me,
refers to

Body and Soul

Sacraments
are catalysts for
that Reconciliation
of
Body and Soul,
My Sexual and My Spiritual,
Mind, Heart, Gut

for Wholeness,

for Holiness

My theology

Holding still and Listening
Gazing intently, Amazed
Lost in Thought
Movement in my Heart
Looking hard at everything
Seeking the Divine in All

Attention
Seeing all around me, in me
Movement
Coming back to myself
Coming back to the Essence
Knowing Faith
Knowing God knows Why I am
Who I am
Passing out of nothingness into Being

Experiencing myself
Creating
Passing from sin to Grace
Darkness to Light
A Cry from my Heart
Returning to God
to Myself
to the World

Hard Work
Constant Practice
Reading
Dialogue

Investigating Clues
Pondering over words and images
Wanderings in a wordless void
Tossed and Torn
Enormous Enthusiasm
Crossing the Deep
Balancing myself
Groping
Unending Purification
Blades of Understanding

Sharing
Writing
Poem, essay, book
Music
Walking
Sitting
Liturgy
Aware

Questioning
Trust
Birth

God

My theology

Neither Conservative nor Liberal Be

Canonize not

the Wisdom of the Present Moment,

nor

Be enslaved by

the structures and formulations

we have inherited.

Peace

(Love in Action)

is

Conservatively Liberal

and

Liberally Conservative

or

none of the above.

A Normal Part of Life

Death is a normal part of life;

Taking care of those approaching it can be
satisfying even joyful.

We put people through fates
much worse than death,

yet do many crazy things
to people facing the end of life.

Prolonged care of
an elderly Alzheimer's patient
on a ventilator
is burdensome therapy,
done in the name of the patient
(but not for his good)
to salve notions of
the caregivers.

Do we ask,
"What are the goals of the dying person?"
or do we ask,
"What medical treatment should we use?"
By focusing on the narrow,
we miss the opportunity
to make people comfortable

in what time they have left.
We invest in "Futile Care"
missing the chance to provide our loved ones
the opportunity to go with dignity.

We are confused:
A child needs absolute protection
from conception to birth—and thereafter.
A dying person
cannot use protection from death.

Do we truly believe in
Life Hereafter with God,
when we maintain ongoing
burdensome, aggressive, futile therapy
trying to keep one from that Life?

Why is it a surprise
that no one gets out of here alive?
A feeding tube
may carry more burdens for a dying person
than benefits.

Why not simply try to provide

A GOOD DEATH;

Comfort, Pain Control, Prayer, Blessings,
Loved Ones Nearby.

Worst case scenario:

Loved ones dying in severe pain
after aggressive and excruciating treatment
with Loved Ones fighting
with each other
and with doctors.

Futile Care and life ending pain
are often the result
of family members
trying to prove their love
by making up for all they did not do
during their lifetime,
expressing Love
through
technology, power, or money.

Many doctors have had
NO TRAINING
on end-of-life comfort.

There will always be suffering
when a Loved One is leaving us;
Not knowing what's on other side
hurts.
We should not focus on legal issues;
We should not react out of fear;
We should not shove tubes
down their throats
when they are dying.

On Meditation

Meditation is a Love Affair.

Love is
the most powerful energy in the Universe.

The irony of meditation
is that through it
I become more immersed in
the here and now.

When I free myself from my ego,
I begin to know and Love others
at a deeper level of awareness.

I find true Compassion.

Through meditation
I gain an inner eye to
the suffering of others
and
the strength
to answer the call to help.

All prayer must lead
Outward
to others.

Meditation and Contemplative Prayer
are a reservoir of Spiritual Vitality
that pours itself out
helping others.

Meditation
awakens
the eye of my heart,
the eye of Love.

This is
Metanoia,
Transformation.